# INVITATION TO VERSE

# INVITATION TO VERSE

*AN ANTHOLOGY*

*selected by*
A. E. M. BAYLISS

*Granger Index Reprint Series*

**BOOKS FOR LIBRARIES PRESS**
FREEPORT, NEW YORK

First published 1943 by George G. Harrap & Co., Ltd.

Reprinted 1971 by arrangement

INTERNATIONAL STANDARD BOOK NUMBER:
0-8369-6280-X


LIBRARY OF CONGRESS CATALOG CARD NUMBER:
72-167475


PRINTED IN THE UNITED STATES OF AMERICA

# FOREWORD

THE poems in this collection are intended for pupils aged ten to thirteen or fourteen. I am aware that three or four years may seem a long period to be covered by a single book, but this particular period of school life presents acute problems to the teacher in the selection of literary material. One of these problems is that of *mental* age, which varies considerably in children who possess the same chronological age, and who may even be taught in the same class. Any attempt to solve it must take into account not only a wide range of juvenile interests but also wide differences in intelligence. Comprehension must precede appreciation.

Bearing these facts in mind, I have tried to gather in one volume an extremely varied collection of verse in which *incident* is the essential feature. In many respects the result is similar to my *Poems of Adventure*, but here I am catering for younger pupils who have not yet outgrown their liking for nonsense stories, magic and make-believe, and other simplicities of narrative verse. Moreover, the passing of peace and the plunging of our nation into war again have seemed to make it more than ever fitting to introduce some of the finest poetry evoked by patriotic sentiment. This will be found in the section entitled "This England."

It need hardly be suggested that the harder

poems should be read aloud *to* the children. Only thus can the elements of rhythm, feeling, imagery, and thought be presented simultaneously to promote complete enjoyment.

Many of the items in this collection have been chosen by my own junior pupils, whose helpful co-operation I acknowledge with gratitude.

A. E. M. B.

# ACKNOWLEDGMENTS

THE editor's thanks are tendered to Mrs George Bambridge and Messrs Methuen and Co., Ltd., for Rudyard Kipling's "For All We Have and Are," from *The Years Between*; to Mr Hilaire Belloc and Messrs Gerald Duckworth and Co., Ltd., for "Matilda," from *Cautionary Tales*; to Messrs Ernest Benn, Ltd., for "Two Sparrows," from *Kensington Gardens*, by Humbert Wolfe; to Mrs Binyon and the Society of Authors for "John Winter," from *London Visions*, by the late Laurence Binyon; to Messrs Jonathan Cape, Ltd., for "Sheep," from *Songs of Joy*, by W. H. Davies; to Mr Walter de la Mare and Messrs Faber and Faber, Ltd., for "The Three Beggars" and "The Englishman," from *Songs of Childhood*; to Mr T. S. Eliot and Messrs Faber and Faber, Ltd., for "Macavity: the Mystery Cat," from *Old Possum's Book of Practical Cats*; to Dr S. Taylor Harris for "Peggy Leg"; to Dr S. Taylor Harris and Messrs J. Curwen and Sons, Ltd., for a slightly adapted version of "The Plank"; to Mr P. E. Herrick for "The Clerk of the Weather"; to Miss Pamela Hinkson for "Modereen Rue," from *The Wind in the Trees*, by Katharine Tynan Hinkson; to the Houghton Mifflin Company, for "The Height of the Ridiculous" and "The Ballad of the Oysterman," by Oliver Wendell Holmes, and "The Blind Men and the Elephant," by J. G. Saxe; to Messrs John Lane (The

Bodley Head), Ltd., for "Clean Clara," from *Lilliput Levee*, by W. B. Rands; to Messrs Longmans, Green and Co., Ltd., for "Willow the King," from *Harrow Songs*, by E. E. Bowen; to Mr Edward MacDuff and Messrs Samuel French, Ltd., for "Ed. and Sid and Bernard," from *Hearthrug Rhymes*; to the author's executors and Messrs Macmillan and Co., Ltd., for "The Walrus and the Carpenter," from *Through the Looking Glass*, by Lewis Carroll; to the author's executors and Messrs John Murray for "The Song of the Bow," from *Songs of Action*, by Sir Arthur Conan Doyle; to Mr Alfred Noyes and Messrs William Blackwood and Sons, for "Sherwood" and "The Admiral's Ghost," from *The Collected Poems of Alfred Noyes*; to Messrs Kegan Paul, Trench, Trübner and Co., Ltd., for "David Gwyn," by Sir Lewis Morris; to Messrs Frederick Warne and Co., Ltd., for "The Dong with a Luminous Nose" and "The Two Bachelors," from *Nonsense Songs and Stories*, by Edward Lear; to Mrs W. B. Yeats and Messrs Macmillan and Co., Ltd., for "The Ballad of Father Gilligan," from *The Collected Poems of W. B. Yeats*.

"England, my England," is reprinted from *Poems*, by W. E. Henley, by permission of the author's executors and Messrs Macmillan and Co., Ltd.; "The Tarry Buccaneer" is reprinted from *Collected Poems of John Masefield* (Wm. Heinemann, Ltd.), by permission of the author ; "Vitaï Lampada" and "Drake's Drum" are reprinted from *Poems New and Old* (Messrs John Murray), by permission of the executors of the late Sir Henry Newbolt; "The Shark" and "The Seven Little Tigers and the Agèd Cook" are reprinted from *Tirra Lirra*, by Laura E. Richards, by permission of Messrs George G. Harrap and Co., Ltd.; "Heather Ale," by Robert Louis Stevenson, is reprinted by permission of Lloyd Osbourne, Esq.; "The Ballad of Semmerwater," from *The Poems of Sir William Watson, 1878–1935*, is included by permission of Messrs George G. Harrap and Co., Ltd.

# CONTENTS

## *NONSENSE NUMBERS*

## *BEASTS AND BIRDS*

PAGE

## THE SALT SEA

## FLIGHTS OF FANCY

## VARIOUS ADVENTURES

## A MEDLEY OF MIRTH

## WONDER AND MAGIC

## ECHOES OF HISTORY

## TRAGIC TALES

# NONSENSE NUMBERS

## THE HEIGHT OF THE RIDICULOUS

I WROTE some lines once on a time
In wondrous merry mood,
And thought, as usual, men would say
They were exceeding good.

They were so queer, so very queer,
I laughed as I would die;
Albeit, in the general way,
A sober man am I.

I called my servant, and he came;
How kind it was of him,
To mind a slender man like me,
He of the mighty limb!

He took the paper, and I watched,
And saw him peep within;
At the first line he read, his face
Was all upon the grin.

He read the next; the grin grew broad,
And shot from ear to ear;
He read the third; a chuckling noise
I now began to hear.

The fourth; he burst into a roar;
The fifth; his waistband split;
The sixth; he burst five buttons off,
And tumbled in a fit.

Ten days and nights, with sleepless eye,
I watched that wretchèd man,
And since, I never dare to write
As funny as I can.

*Oliver Wendell Holmes*

### THE TWINS

In form and feature, face and limb,
    I grew so like my brother,
That folks got taking me for him,
    And each for one another.
It puzzled all our kith and kin,
    It reached a fearful pitch,
For one of us was born a twin,
    Yet not a soul knew which.

One day, to make the matter worse,
    Before our names were fixed,
As we were being washed by nurse,
    We got completely mixed;
And thus you see, by fate's decree,
    Or rather nurse's whim,
My brother John got christened *me*,
    And I got christened *him*.

This fatal likeness even dogged
    My footsteps when at school,
And I was always getting flogged,
    For John turned out a fool.

I put this question fruitlessly
   To every one I knew,
"What *would* you do, if you were me,
   To prove that you were *you* ?"

Our close resemblance turned the tide
   Of my domestic life,
For somehow, my intended bride
   Became my brother's wife.
In fact, year after year, the same
   Absurd mistakes went on,
And when I died, the neighbours came
   And buried brother John.

                 *H. S. Leigh*

## THE BLIND MEN AND THE ELEPHANT

### *A Hindoo Fable*

It was six men of Indostan,
   To learning much inclined,
Who went to see the Elephant
   (Though all of them were blind),
That each by observation
   Might satisfy his mind.

The *First* approached the Elephant,
   And happening to fall
Against his broad and sturdy side,
   At once began to bawl:
"God bless me, but the Elephant
   Is very like a wall!"

The *Second*, feeling of the tusk,
  Cried, "Ho! what have we here
So very round and smooth and sharp?
  To me 'tis mighty clear
This wonder of an Elephant
  Is very like a spear!"


The *Third* approached the animal,
  And happening to take
The squirming trunk within his hands,
  Thus boldly up and spake:
"I see," quoth he, "the Elephant
  Is very like a snake!"


The *Fourth* stretched out an eager hand,
  And felt about the knee.
"What most this wondrous beast is like
  Is mighty plain," quoth he;
"'Tis clear enough the Elephant
  Is very like a tree!"


The *Fifth*, who chanced to touch the ear,
  Said: "E'en the blindest man
Can tell what this resembles most;
  Deny the fact who can,
This marvel of an Elephant
  Is very like a fan!"


The *Sixth* no sooner had begun
  About the beast to grope,
Than, seizing on the swinging tail
  That fell within his scope,

"I see," quoth he, "the Elephant
  Is very like a rope!"


And so these men of Indostan
  Disputed loud and long,
Each in his own opinion
  Exceeding stiff and strong,
Though each was partly in the right,
  And all were in the wrong!

*John G. Saxe*


A WARNING

THREE children sliding on the ice
  Upon a summer's day,
It so fell out they all fell in;
  The rest they ran away.


Now, had these children been at home,
  Or sliding on dry ground,
Ten thousand pounds to one penny
  They had not all been drowned.


You parents all that children have,
  And you that have got none,
If you would have them safe abroad,
  Pray keep them safe at home.

*John Gay*

### THE WISE MEN OF GOTHAM

In a bowl to sea went wise men three,
   On a brilliant night of June;
They carried a net, and their hearts were set
   On fishing up the moon.

The sea was calm, the air was balm,
   Not a breath stirred low or high,
And the moon, I trow, lay as bright below,
   And as round as in the sky.

The wise men with the current went
   Nor paddle nor oar had they,
And still as the grave they went on the wave,
   That they might not disturb their prey.

Far, far at sea, were the wise men three,
   When their fishing-net they threw;
And at the throw, the moon below
   In a thousand fragments flew.

The sea was bright with a dancing light
   Of a million million gleams,
Which the broken moon shot forth as soon
   As the net disturbed her beams.

They drew in their net; it was empty and wet,
   And they had lost their pain;
Soon ceased the play of each dancing ray,
   And the image was round again.

Three times they threw, three times they drew,
  And all the while were mute;
And evermore their wonder grew,
  Till they could not but dispute.

Their silence they broke, and each one spoke
  Full long, and loud, and clear;
A man at sea their voices three
  Full three leagues off might hear.

The three wise men got home again
  To their children and their wives;
But, touching their trip, and their net's vain dip,
  They disputed all their lives.

The wise men three could never agree,
  Why they missed the promised boon;
They agreed alone that their net they had thrown,
  And they had not caught the moon.

*T. L. Peacock*

### THE SHARK

OH! blithe and merrily sang the shark,
  As he sat on the house-top high:
A-cleaning his boots, and smoking cheroots,
  With a single glass in his eye.

With Martin and Day he polished away,
  And a smile on his face did glow,
As merry and bold the chorus he trolled
  Of "Gobble-em-upsky ho!"

He sang so loud, he astonished the crowd
   Which gathered from far and near.
For they said, "Such a sound, in the country round,
   We never, no, never did hear."

He sang of the ships that he'd eaten like chips
   In the palmy days of his youth.
And he added, "If you don't believe it is true,
   Pray examine my wisdom tooth!"

He sang of the whales who'd have given their tails
   For a glance of his raven eye.
And the swordfish, too, who their weapons all
     drew,
   And swor'd for his sake they'd die.

And he sang about wrecks and hurricane decks
   And the mariner's perils and pains,
Till every man's blood up on end it stood,
   And their hair ran cold in their veins.

But blithe as a lark the merry old shark,
   He sat on the sloping roof.
Though he said, "It is queer that no one draws
     near
   To examine my wisdom toof!"

And he carolled away, by night and by day,
   Until he made every one ill.
And I'll wager a crown that unless he's come
     down,
   He is probably carolling still.

*Laura E. Richards*

### THE SEVEN LITTLE TIGERS AND THE AGÈD COOK

SEVEN little tigers they sat them in a row,
Their seven little dinners for to eat;
And each of the troop had a little plate of soup
The effect of which was singularly neat.

They were feeling rather cross, for they hadn't any
    sauce
To eat with their pudding or their pie;
So they rumpled up their hair, in a spasm of
    despair,
And vowed that the agèd cook should die.

Then they called the agèd cook, and a frying-pan
    they took,
To fry him very nicely for their supper;
He was ninety-six years old, on authority I'm told,
And his name was Peter Sparrow-piper Tupper.

"Mr Sparrow-piper Tup, we intend on you to
    sup!"
Said the eldest little tiger very sweetly;
But this naughty agèd cook, just remarking,
    "Only look!"
Chopped the little tiger's head off very neatly.

Then he said unto the rest, "It has always been
    confessed
That a tiger's better eating than a man;
So I'll fry him for you now, and you all will find,
    I trow,
That to eat him will be much the better plan."

So they tried it in a trice, and found that it was
    nice,
And with rapture they embracèd one another;
And they said, "By hook or crook, we must keep
    this agèd cook;
So we'll ask him to become our elder brother."
                         [*Which they accordingly did.*]

                              *Laura E. Richards*

## THE WALRUS AND THE CARPENTER

THE sun was shining on the sea,
Shining with all his might:
He did his very best to make
The billows smooth and bright—
And this was odd, because it was
The middle of the night.

The moon was shining sulkily,
Because she thought the sun
Had got no business to be there
After the day was done—
"It's very rude of him," she said,
"To come and spoil the fun!"

The sea was wet as wet could be,
The sands were dry as dry.
You could not see a cloud, because
No cloud was in the sky:
No birds were flying overhead—
There were no birds to fly.

The Walrus and the Carpenter
Were walking close at hand:
They wept like anything to see
Such quantities of sand:
"If this were only cleared away,"
They said, "it *would* be grand!"

"If seven maids with seven mops
Swept it for half a year,
Do you suppose," the Walrus said,
"That they could get it clear?"
"I doubt it," said the Carpenter,
And shed a bitter tear.

"O Oysters, come and walk with us!"
The Walrus did beseech.
"A pleasant walk, a pleasant talk,
Along the briny beach:
We cannot do with more than four,
To give a hand to each."

The eldest Oyster looked at him;
But never a word he said:
The eldest Oyster winked his eye,
And shook his heavy head—
Meaning to say he did not choose
To leave the oyster-bed.

But four young Oysters hurried up,
All eager for the treat:
Their coats were brushed, their faces washed,
Their shoes were clean and neat—
And this was odd, because, you know,
They hadn't any feet.

Four other Oysters followed them,
And yet another four;
And thick and fast they came at last,
And more, and more, and more—
All hopping through the frothy waves,
And scrambling to the shore.

The Walrus and the Carpenter
Walked on a mile or so,
And then they rested on a rock
Conveniently low:
And all the little Oysters stood
And waited in a row.

"The time has come," the Walrus said,
"To talk of many things:
Of shoes—and ships—and sealing-wax—
Of cabbages—and kings—
And why the sea is boiling hot—
And whether pigs have wings."

"But wait a bit," the Oysters cried,
"Before we have our chat;
For some of us are out of breath,
And all of us are fat!"
"No hurry!" said the Carpenter.
They thanked him much for that.

"A loaf of bread," the Walrus said,
"Is what we chiefly need:
Pepper and vinegar besides
Are very good indeed—
Now, if you're ready, Oysters dear,
We can begin to feed."

"But not on us!" the Oysters cried,
Turning a little blue.
"After such kindness, that would be
A dismal thing to do!"
"The night is fine," the Walrus said.
"Do you admire the view?

"It was so kind of you to come!
And you are very nice!"
The Carpenter said nothing but
"Cut us another slice.
I wish you were not quite so deaf—
I've had to ask you twice!"

"It seems a shame," the Walrus said,
"To play them such a trick,
After we've brought them out so far,
And made them trot so quick!"
The Carpenter said nothing but
"The butter's spread too thick!"

"I weep for you," the Walrus said:
"I deeply sympathize."
With sobs and tears he sorted out
Those of the largest size,
Holding his pocket-handkerchief
Before his streaming eyes.

"O Oysters," said the Carpenter,
"You've had a pleasant run!
Shall we be trotting home again?"
But answer came there none—
And this was scarcely odd, because
They'd eaten every one.

*Lewis Carroll*

### YOU ARE OLD, FATHER WILLIAM

"You are old, Father William," the young man
    said,
  "And your hair has become very white;
And yet you incessantly stand on your head—
  Do you think, at your age, it is right?"

"In my youth," Father William replied to his son,
  "I feared it might injure the brain;
But, now that I'm perfectly sure I have none,
  Why, I do it again and again."

"You are old," said the youth, "as I mentioned
    before,
  And have grown most uncommonly fat;
Yet you turned a back-somersault in at the door—
  Pray, what is the reason of that?"

"In my youth," said the sage, as he shook his
    grey locks,
  "I kept all my limbs very supple
By the use of this ointment—one shilling the box—
  Allow me to sell you a couple?"

"You are old," said the youth, "and your jaws
    are too weak
  For anything tougher than suet;
Yet you finished the goose, with the bones and
    the beak—
  Pray, how did you manage to do it?"

"In my youth," said his father, "I took to the law,
  And argued each case with my wife;
And the muscular strength which it gave to my
    jaw
  Has lasted the rest of my life."


"You are old," said the youth, "one would hardly
    suppose
  That your eye was as steady as ever;
Yet you balanced an eel on the end of your nose—
  What made you so awfully clever?"


"I have answered three questions, and that is
    enough,"
  Said his father; "don't give yourself airs!
Do you think I can listen all day to such stuff?
  Be off, or I'll kick you downstairs!"

*Lewis Carroll*


### THE DONG WITH A LUMINOUS NOSE

WHEN awful darkness and silence reign
Over the great Gromboolian plain,
  Through the long, long, wintry nights;
    When the angry breakers roar,
    As they beat on the rocky shore;
  When Storm-clouds brood on the towering
    heights
    Of the Hills of the Chankly Bore:

Then, through the vast and gloomy dark,
There moves what seems a fiery spark,
 A lonely spark with silvery rays
  Piercing the coal-black night,
  A meteor strange and bright:
 Hither and thither the vision strays,
  A single lurid light.

Slowly it wanders—pauses—creeps—
Anon it sparkles—flashes and leaps;
And ever as onward it gleaming goes
A light on the Bong-tree stems it throws.
And those who watch at that midnight hour
From Hall, or Terrace, or lofty Tower,
Cry, as the wild light passes along,
   "The Dong!—the Dong!
The wandering Dong through the forest goes!
   The Dong!—the Dong!
The Dong with a luminous Nose!"

  Long years ago
 The Dong was happy and gay,
Till he fell in love with a Jumbly Girl
 Who came to those shores one day.
For the Jumblies came in a Sieve, they did,
Landing at eve near the Zemmery Fidd
  Where the Oblong Oysters grow,
 And the rocks are smooth and grey.
And all the woods and the valleys rang
With the Chorus they daily and nightly sang—
 *"Far and few, far and few,*
  *Are the lands where the Jumblies live;*
  *Their heads are green and their hands are blue,*
  *And they went to sea in a sieve."*

Happily, happily passed those days!
    While the cheerful Jumblies staid;
    They danced in circlets all night long,
    To the plaintive pipe of the lively Dong,
        In the moonlight, shine or shade.
For day and night he was always there
By the side of the Jumbly Girl so fair,
With her sky-blue hands, and her sea-green
    hair.
Till the morning came of that hateful day
When the Jumblies sailed in their sieve away,
And the Dong was left on the cruel shore
Gazing—gazing for evermore,
Ever keeping his weary eyes on
That pea-green sail on the far horizon,
Singing the Jumbly Chorus still
As he sate all day on the grassy hill—
    "*Far and few, far and few,*
        *Are the lands where the Jumblies live;*
        *Their heads are green, and their hands are blue,*
        *And they went to sea in a sieve.*"


But when the sun was low in the West,
    The Dong arose and said,
    "What little sense I once possessed
    Has quite gone out of my head!"
And since that day he wanders still
By lake and forest, marsh and hill,
Singing—"O somewhere, in valley or plain
Might I find my Jumbly Girl again!
For ever I'll seek by lake and shore
Till I find my Jumbly Girl once more!"

Playing a pipe with silvery squeaks,
Since then his Jumbly Girl he seeks.
And because by night he could not see,
He gathered the bark of the Twangum
    Tree
  On the flowery plain that grows.
  And he wove him a wondrous Nose—
A Nose as strange as a Nose could be!

Of vast proportions, and painted red,
And tied with cords to the back of his head.
    —In a hollow rounded space it ended
  With a luminous lamp within suspended,
    All fenced about
    With a bandage stout
  To prevent the wind from blowing it out;
And with holes all round to send the light,
In gleaming rays on the dismal night.

And now each night, and all night long,
Over those plains still roams the Dong;
And above the wail of the Chimp and Snipe
You may hear the squeak of his plaintive
    pipe
While ever he seeks, but seeks in vain
To meet with his Jumbly Girl again;
Lonely and wild—all night he goes—
The Dong with a luminous Nose!
And all who watch at the midnight hour,
From Hall, or Terrace, or lofty Tower,
Cry, as they trace the Meteor bright,
Moving along through the dreary night,

"This is the hour when forth he goes,
The Dong with a luminous Nose!
Yonder—over the plain he goes;
   He goes!
   He goes;
The Dong with a luminous Nose!"

*Edward Lear*

# BEASTS AND BIRDS

## SHEEP

When I was once in Baltimore
  A man came up to me and cried,
"Come, I have eighteen hundred sheep,
  And we will sail on Tuesday's tide.

"If you will sail with me, young man,
  I'll pay you fifty shillings down;
These eighteen hundred sheep I take
  From Baltimore to Glasgow town."

He paid me fifty shillings down,
  I sailed with eighteen hundred sheep;
We soon had cleared the harbour's mouth,
  We soon were in the salt sea deep.

The first night we were out at sea
  Those sheep were quiet in their mind;
The second night they cried with fear—
  They smelt no pastures in the wind.

They sniffed, poor things, for their green fields,
  They cried so loud I could not sleep:
For fifty thousand shillings down
  I would not sail again with sheep.

*W. H. Davies*

## THE MOUNTAIN AND THE SQUIRREL

The Mountain and the Squirrel
Had a quarrel,
And the former called the latter "Little Prig";
Bun replied,
"You are doubtless very big;
But all sorts of things and weather
Must be taken in together
To make up a year
And a sphere.
And I think it no disgrace
To occupy my place.
If I'm not so large as you,
You are not so small as I,
And not half so spry.
I'll not deny you make
A very pretty squirrel track.
Talents differ; all is well and wisely put;
If I cannot carry forests on my back
Neither can you crack a nut."

*Ralph Waldo Emerson*

## EPITAPH ON A HARE

Here lies, whom hound did ne'er pursue,
   Nor swifter greyhound follow,
Whose foot ne'er tainted morning dew,
   Nor ear heard huntsman hallo;

Old Tiney, surliest of his kind,
　Who, nursed with tender care,
And to domestic bounds confined,
　Was still a wild Jack-hare.

Though duly from my hand he took
　His pittance ev'ry night,
He did it with a jealous look,
　And, when he could, would bite.

His diet was of wheaten bread,
　And milk, and oats, and straw;
Thistles, or lettuces instead,
　With sand to scour his maw.

On twigs of hawthorn he regaled,
　On pippins' russet peel;
And, when his juicy salads failed,
　Sliced carrot pleased him well.

A Turkey carpet was his lawn,
　Whereon he loved to bound,
To skip and gambol like a fawn,
　And swing his rump around.

His frisking was at evening hours,
　For then he lost his fear;
But most before approaching showers,
　Or when a storm drew near.

Eight years and five round-rolling moons
　He thus saw steal away,
Dozing out all his idle noons,
　And every night at play.

I kept him for his humour's sake,
    For he would oft beguile
My heart of thoughts that made it ache,
    And force me to a smile.

But now, beneath this walnut-shade
    He finds his long, last home,
And waits in snug concealment laid,
    'Till gentler Puss shall come.

He, still more agèd, feels the shocks
    From which no care can save,
And, partner once of Tiney's box,
    Must soon partake his grave.

*William Cowper*

## MODEREEN RUE [1]

Och, Modereen Rue, you little red rover,
By the glint of the moon you stole out of your
    cover,
And now there is never an egg to be got,
Nor a handsome fat chicken to put in the pot.
    Och, Modereen Rue!

With your nose to the earth and your ear on the
    listen,
You slunk through the stubble with frost-drops
    a-glisten,

[1] *I.e.*, the little red rogue—the fox.

With my lovely fat drake in your teeth as you went,
That your red roguish children should breakfast
content.
       Och; Modereen Rue!

Och, Modereen Rue, hear the horn for a warning,
They are looking for red roguish foxes this morn-
ing;
But let them come my way, you little red rogue,
'Tis I will betray you to huntsman and dog.
       Och, Modereen Rue!

The little red rogue, he's the colour of bracken,
O'er mountains, o'er valleys, his pace will not
slacken.
Tantara! tantara! he is off now, and, faith!
'Tis a race 'twixt the little red rogue and his death.
       Och, Modereen Rue!

Och, Modereen Rue, I've no cause to be grieving
For little red rogues and their tricks and their
thieving,
The hounds they give tongue, and the quarry's in
sight,
The hens on the roost may sleep easy to-night.
       Och, Modereen Rue!

But my blessing be on him. He made the hounds
follow
Through the woods, through the dales, over hill,
over hollow,
It was Modereen Rue led them fast, led them far,
From the glint of the morning till eve's silver star.
       Och, Modereen Rue!

And he saved his red brush for his own future
    wearing,
He slipped into a drain, and he left the hounds
    swearing.
Good luck, my fine fellow, and long may you show
Such a clean pair of heels to the hounds as they go.
      Och, Modereen Rue!

*Katharine Tynan Hinkson*

## POOR OLD HORSE

ONCE I was clothed in linsey woolsey fine,
My mane it did hang down, and my coat it did
    shine,
But now I'm growing old, and nature doth decay,
My master frowns on me, and these words I heard
    him say,
      "Poor old horse! You must die!"

I used to be kept all in the stable warm,
I had the best of shelter from cold and rain and
    harm;
But now in open meadow, a hedge I'm glad to find,
To shield my sides from tempest, from driving
    sleet and wind.
      Poor old horse, let him die!

My shoulders once were sturdy, were glossy,
    smooth and round,
But now, alas! they're rotten, I'm not accounted
    sound.

As I have grown so agèd, my teeth gone to decay,
My master frowns upon me; I often hear him say,
    "Poor old horse, let him die!"

A groom upon me waited, on straw I snugly lay,
When fields were full of flowers, the air was sweet
    with hay;
But now there's no good feeding prepared for me
    at all,
I'm forced to munch the nettles upon the kennel
    wall.
        Poor old horse, let him die!

My hide unto the huntsman so freely I will give,
My body to the hounds, for I'd rather die than
    live;
I've followed them full often, ay! many a score of
    miles,
O'er hedges, walls, and ditches, nor blinked at
    gates and stiles.
        Poor old horse!  You must die!

Ye gentlemen of England, ye sportsmen good and
    bold,
All ye that love a hunter, remember him when
    old;
Oh, put him in your stable, and make the old boy
    warm,
And visit him, and pat him, and keep him out of
    harm,
        Poor old horse, till he die.

*Anonymous*

### LLEWELLYN AND HIS DOG

THE spearman heard the bugle sound,
  And cheerly smiled the morn;
And many a brach, and many a hound,
  Obeyed Llewellyn's horn.

And still he blew a louder blast,
  And gave a louder cheer:
"Come, Gelert, come, wert never last
  Llewellyn's horn to hear!

"Oh, where does faithful Gelert roam?
  The flower of all his race!
So true, so brave—a lamb at home,
  A lion in the chase!"

That day Llewellyn little loved
  The chase of hart or hare;
And scant and small the booty proved,
  For Gelert was not there.

Unpleased Llewellyn homeward hied,
  When, near the portal-seat,
His truant, Gelert, he espied,
  Bounding his lord to greet.

But when he gained his castle-door,
  Aghast the chieftain stood;
The hound all o'er was smeared with gore—
  His lips, his fangs ran blood!

Llewellyn gazed with fierce surprise,
   Unused such looks to meet,
His favourite checked his joyful guise,
   And crouched and licked his feet.

Onward in haste Llewellyn passed—
   And on went Gelert too—
And still, where'er his eyes were cast,
   Fresh blood-gouts shocked his view!

O'erturned his infant's bed he found,
   The bloodstained covert rent,
And all around, the walls and ground,
   With recent blood besprent.

He called his child—no voice replied;
   He searched—with terror wild;
Blood! blood! he found on every side,
   But nowhere found the child!

"Hell-hound! my child's by thee devoured!"
   The frantic father cried;
And, to the hilt, his vengeful sword
   He plunged in Gelert's side!

His suppliant looks, as prone he fell,
   No pity could impart;
But still his Gelert's dying yell,
   Passed heavy o'er his heart.

Aroused by Gelert's dying yell,
   Some slumberer wakened nigh;
What words the parent's joy can tell,
   To hear his infant cry?

Concealed beneath a tumbled heap,
  His hurried search had missed,
All glowing from his rosy sleep
  The cherub-boy he kissed.

Nor scathe had he, nor harm, nor dread;
  But the same couch beneath
Lay a gaunt wolf, all torn and dead—
  Tremendous still in death!

Ah! what was then Llewellyn's pain,
  For now the truth was clear:
The gallant hound the wolf had slain,
  To save Llewellyn's heir.

Vain, vain was all Llewellyn's woe;
  "Best of thy kind, adieu!
The frantic deed which laid thee low
  This heart shall ever rue!"

And now a gallant tomb they raise,
  With costly sculpture decked;
And marbles, storied with his praise,
  Poor Gelert's bones protect.

Here never could the spearman pass,
  Or forester, unmoved;
Here oft the tear-besprinkled grass
  Llewellyn's sorrow proved.

And here he hung his horn and spear,
  And there, as evening fell,
In fancy's ear he oft would hear
  Poor Gelert's dying yell.

*W. R. Spencer*

### MACAVITY: THE MYSTERY CAT

Macavity's a Mystery Cat: he's called the Hidden
    Paw—
For he's the master criminal who can defy the
    Law.
He's the bafflement of Scotland Yard, the Flying
    Squad's despair:
For when they reach the scene of crime—
    "Macavity's not there!"

Macavity, Macavity, there's no one like Macavity,
He's broken every human law, he breaks the law
    of gravity.
His powers of levitation would make a fakir stare,
And when you reach the scene of crime—
    "Macavity's not there!"
You may seek him in the basement, you may look
    up in the air—
But I tell you once and once again, "Macavity's
    not there!"

Macavity's a ginger cat; he's very tall and thin;
You would know him if you saw him, for his eyes
    are sunken in.
His brow is deeply lined with thought, his head
    is highly domed;
His coat is dusty from neglect, his whiskers are
    uncombed.
He sways his head from side to side, with move-
    ments like a snake;
And when you think he's half asleep, he's always
    wide awake.

Macavity, Macavity, there's no one like Macavity,
For he's a fiend in feline shape, a monster of
    depravity.
You may meet him in a by-street, you may see
    him in the square—
But when a crime's discovered, then "Macavity's
    not there!"

He's outwardly respectable. (They say he cheats
    at cards.)
And his footprints are not found in any file of
    Scotland Yard's.
And when the larder's looted, or the jewel-case
    is rifled,
Or when the milk is missing, or another Peke's
    been stifled,
Or the greenhouse glass is broken, and the trellis
    past repair—
Ay, there's the wonder of the thing! "Macavity's
    not there!"

And when the Foreign Office find a Treaty's gone
    astray,
Or the Admiralty lose some plans and drawings
    by the way,
There may be a scrap of paper in the hall or on
    the stair—
But it's useless to investigate—"Macavity's not
    there!"
And when the loss has been disclosed, the Secret
    Service say:
"It MUST have been Macavity!"—but he's half a
    mile away.

You'll be sure to find him resting, or a-licking of
    his thumbs,
Or engaged in doing complicated long division
    sums.

Macavity, Macavity, there's no one like Macavity,
There never was a Cat of such deceitfulness and
    suavity.
He always has an alibi, and one or two to spare:
At whatever time the deed took place—MACAVITY
    WASN'T THERE!
And they say that all the Cats whose wicked deeds
    are widely known
(I might mention Mungojerrie, I might mention
    Griddlebone)
Are nothing more than agents for the Cat who
    all the time
Just controls their operations: the Napoleon of
    Crime!

*T. S. Eliot*

### THE PARROT

A PARROT from the Spanish main,
    Full young and early caged, came o'er,
With bright wings, to the bleak domain
    Of Mullah's shore.

To spicy groves where he had won
    His plumage of resplendent hue,
His native fruits, and skies, and sun,
    He bade adieu.

For these he changed the smoke of turf,
  A heathery land and misty sky,
And turned on rocks and raging surf
  His golden eye.

But petted in our climate cold,
  He lived and chattered many a day,
Until with age, from green and gold
  His wings grew grey.

At last when blind, and seeming dumb,
  He scolded, laughed, and spoke no more,
A Spanish stranger chanced to come
  To Mullah's shore;

He hailed the bird in Spanish speech,
  The bird in Spanish speech replied;
Flapp'd round the cage with joyous screech,
  Dropped down, and died.

*Thomas Campbell*

### TWO SPARROWS

Two sparrows, feeding,
heard a thrush
sing to the dawn.
The first said "Tush!

In all my life
I never heard
a more affected
singing-bird."

The second said
"It's you and me,
who slave to keep
the likes of he."

"And if we cared,"
both sparrows said,
"we'd do that singing
on our head."

The thrush pecked sideways,
and was dumb.
"And now," they screamed,
"he's pinched our crumb."

*Humbert Wolfe*

## THE JACKDAW OF RHEIMS

THE Jackdaw sat on the Cardinal's chair:
Bishop and abbot and prior were there;
  Many a monk, and many a friar,
  Many a knight, and many a squire,
With a great many more of lesser degree—
In sooth, a goodly company;
And they served the Lord Primate on bended
    knee.
  Never, I ween,
  Was a prouder seen,
Read of in books, or dreamt of in dreams,
Than the Cardinal Lord Archbishop of Rheims!

In and out,
Through the motley rout,
That little Jackdaw kept hopping about;
Here and there,
Like a dog in a fair,
Over comfits and cakes,
And dishes and plates,
Cowl and cope, and rochet and pall,
Mitre and crosier—he hopp'd upon all!
With saucy air,
He perch'd on the chair
Where, in state, the great Lord Cardinal sat
In the great Lord Cardinal's great red hat;
And he peer'd in the face
Of his Lordship's Grace,
With a satisfied look, as if he would say,
"We two are the greatest folks here to-day!"
And the priests, with awe,
As such freaks they saw.
Said, "The Devil must be in that little Jackdaw!"

The feast was over, the board was cleared,
The flawns and the custards had all disappeared,
And six little singing boys—dear little souls,
In nice clean faces, and nice white stoles—
Came in order due,
Two by two,
Marching that grand refectory through.
A nice little boy held a golden ewer,
Embossed and filled with water, as pure
As any that flows between Rheims and Namur,
Which a nice little boy stood ready to catch
In a fine golden hand-basin made to match.

D

Two nice little boys, rather more grown,
Carried lavender-water and eau-de-Cologne;
And a nice little boy had a nice cake of soap,
Worthy of washing the hands of the Pope.
    One little boy more
    A napkin bore,
Of the best white diaper, fringed with pink,
And a Cardinal's hat marked in "permanent ink."

The great Lord Cardinal turns at the sight
Of these nice little boys dressed all in white:
    From his finger he draws
    His costly turquoise;
And, not thinking at all about little Jackdaws,
    Deposits it straight
    By the side of his plate,
While the nice little boys on his Eminence wait;
Till, when nobody's dreaming of any such thing,
That little Jackdaw hops off with the ring!

    There's a cry and a shout,
    And a deuce of a rout,
And nobody seems to know what they're about,
But the monks have their pockets all turned inside
        out;
    The friars are kneeling,
    And hunting, and feeling
The carpet, the floor, and the walls, and the
        ceiling.
    The Cardinal drew
    Off each plum-coloured shoe,
And left his red stockings exposed to the view;
    He peeps, and he feels
    In the toes and the heels;

They turn up the dishes—they turn up the plates—
They take up the poker and poke out the grates,
  —They turn up the rugs,
  They examine the mugs:
  But no!—no such thing;
  They can't find THE RING!
And the Abbot declared that, "when nobody
    twigged it,
Some rascal or other had popped in, and prigged
    it!"

The Cardinal rose with a dignified look,
He called for his candle, his bell, and his book:
  In holy anger, and pious grief,
  He solemnly cursed that rascally thief!
  He cursed him at board, he cursed him in
    bed,
  From the sole of his foot to the crown of his
    head!
  He cursed him in sleeping, that every night
  He should dream of the devil, and wake in a
    fright;
  He cursed him in eating, he cursed him in
    drinking,
  He cursed him in coughing, in sneezing, in
    winking;
  He cursed him in sitting, in standing, in lying;
  He cursed him in walking, in riding, in flying;
  He cursed him in living, he cursed him in dying!
Never was heard such a terrible curse!
  But what gave rise
  To no little surprise,
Nobody seemed one penny the worse!

The day was gone,
The night came on,
The monks and the friars they searched till
    dawn;
When the sacristan saw,
On crumpled claw
Come limping a poor little lame Jackdaw.
No longer gay,
As on yesterday;
His feathers all seemed to be turned the wrong
    way;
His pinions drooped—he could hardly stand,
His head was as bald as the palm of your hand;
His eyes so dim,
So wasted each limb,
That, heedless of grammar, they all cried, "THAT'S
    HIM!
That's the scamp that has done this scandalous
    thing!
That's the thief that has got my Lord Cardinal's
    Ring!"

The poor little Jackdaw,
When the monks he saw,
Feebly gave vent to the ghost of a caw;
And turned his bald head, as much as to say,
"Pray, be so good as to walk this way!"
Slower and slower
He limped on before,
Till they came to the back of the belfry-door,
Where the first thing they saw,
'Midst the sticks and the straw,
Was the RING in the nest of that little Jackdaw.

Then the great Lord Cardinal called for his
    book,
And off that terrible curse he took;
    The mute expression
    Served in lieu of confession,
    And, being thus coupled with full restitution,
    The Jackdaw got plenary absolution!
    —When those words were heard,
    That poor little bird
Was so changed in a moment, 'twas really absurd.
    He grew sleek and fat;
    In addition to that,
A fresh crop of feathers came thick as a mat.
    His tail waggled more
    Even than before;
But no longer it wagged with an impudent
    air,
No longer he perched on the Cardinal's chair.
    He hopped now about
    With a gait devout;
At Matins, at Vespers, he never was out;
And, so far from any more pilfering deeds,
He always seemed telling the Confessor's beads.
If any one lied, or if any one swore,
Or slumbered in prayer-time, and happened to
    snore,
    That good Jackdaw
    Would give a great "Caw!"
As much as to say, "Don't do so any more!"
While many remarked, as his manners they
    saw,
That they "never had known such a pious
    Jackdaw!"

He long lived the pride
Of that countryside,
And, at last, in the odour of sanctity died;
When, as words were too faint
His merits to paint,
The Conclave determined to make him a Saint;
And on newly-made Saints and Popes, as you know,
It's the custom, at Rome, new names to bestow,
So they canonized him by the name of JIM CROW!

*R. H. Barham*

# THE SALT SEA

A WET sheet and a flowing sea,
  A wind that follows fast,
And fills the white and rustling sail,
  And bends the gallant mast;
And bends the gallant mast, my boys,
  While, like the eagle free,
Away the good ship flies, and leaves
  Old England on the lee.

O for a soft and gentle wind!
  I heard a fair one cry;
But give to me the snoring breeze
  And white waves heaving high;
And white waves heaving high, my boys,
  The good ship tight and free—
The world of waters is our home,
  And merry men are we.

There's tempest in yon hornèd moon,
  And lightning in yon cloud;
But hark the music, mariners!
  The wind is piping loud;
The wind is piping loud, my boys,
  The lightning flashes free—
While the hollow oak our palace is,
  Our heritage the sea.

*Alan Cunningham*

### THE TARRY BUCCANEER

I'M going to be a pirate with a bright brass pivot-
    gun,
And an island in the Spanish Main beyond the
    setting sun,
And a silver flagon full of red wine to drink when
    work is done,
  Like a fine old salt-sea scavenger, like a tarry
    Buccaneer.

With a sandy creek to careen in, and a pig-tailed
    Spanish mate,
And under my main hatches a sparkling merry
    freight
Of doubloons and double moidores, and pieces of
    eight,
  Like a fine old salt-sea scavenger, like a tarry
    Buccaneer.

With a taste for Spanish wine-shops and for spend-
    ing my doubloons,
And a crew of swart mulattoes and black-eyed
    octoroons,
And a thoughtful way with mutineers of making
    them maroons,
  Like a fine old salt-sea scavenger, like a tarry
    Buccaneer.

With a sash of crimson · velvet and a diamond-
    hilted sword,
And a silver whistle about my neck secured to a
    golden cord,

And a habit of taking captives and walking them
    along a board,
  Like a fine old salt-sea scavenger, like a tarry
  Buccaneer.


With a spy-glass tucked beneath my arm and a
    cocked hat cocked askew.
And a long low rakish schooner a-cutting of the
    waves in two,
And a flag of skull and cross-bones the wickedest
    that ever flew,
  Like a fine old salt-sea scavenger, like a tarry
  Buccaneer.

*John Masefield*


### THE PLANK

Did ever ye hear of Bluebeard Joe,
The Pirate grim from Borneo,
Who never would let his prisoners go
Except to Davy Jones by way of the plank,
    The slippery plank,
Except to Davy Jones by way of the plank!


'E were King o' the Main from Ohio
To the Rooshian Archipelago,
And were always reckoned a bit of a beau
Except by those poor chaps who walked 'is plank,
    'Is 'orrible plank,
Except by those poor chaps who walked 'is plank.

'E met old jolly Jack Tar one day.
And 'e roared like the divil, "Belay! belay!"
But 'is ship it were sunk in Botany Bay,
And down went Bluebeard Joe along of 'is plank,
And that were the end of Bluebeard Joe and 'is
  plank!

*S. Taylor Harris*


### JOHN WINTER

WHAT ails John Winter, that so oft
  Silent he sits apart?
The neighbours cast their looks on him;
  But deep he hides his heart.


In Deptford streets the houses small
  Huddle forlorn together.
Whether the wind blow or be still,
  'Tis soiled and sorry weather.


But over these dim roofs arise
  Tall masts of ocean ships.
Whenever John Winter looked at them
  The salt blew on his lips.


He cannot pace the street about,
  But they stand before his eyes!
The more he shuns them, the more proud
  And beautiful they rise.

He turns his head, but in his ear
   The steady Trade Winds run,
And in his eye the endless waves
   Ride on into the sun.

His little child at evening said,
   "Now tell us, dad, a tale
Of naked men that shoot with bows,
   Tell of the spouting whale!"

He told old tales, his eyes were bright,
   His wife looked up to see,
And smiled on him: but in the midst
   He ended suddenly.

He bade his boys good-night, and kissed
   And held them to his breast.
They wondered and were still, to feel
   Their lips so fondly pressed.

He sat absorbed in silent gloom.
   His wife lifted her head
From sewing, and stole up to him,
   "What ails you, John?" she said.

He spoke no word.   A silent tear
   Fell softly down her cheek.
She knelt beside him, and his hand
   Was on her forehead meek.

But even as his tender touch
   Her dumb distress consoled,
The mighty waves danced in his eyes
   And through the silence rolled.

There fell a soft November night,
    Restless with gusts that shook
The chimneys, and beat wildly down
    The flames in the chimney-nook.

John Winter lay beside his wife,
    'Twas past the mid of night.
Softly he rose, and in dead hush
    Stood stealthily upright.

Softly he came where slept his boys,
    And kissed them in their bed;
One stretched his arms out in his sleep:
    At that he turned his head.

And now he bent above his wife,
    She slept a peace serene,
Her patient soul was in the peace
    Of breathing slumber seen.

At last, he kissed one aching kiss,
    Then shrank again in dread,
And from his own home guiltily
    And like a thief he fled.

But now with darkness and the wind
    He breathes a breath more free,
And walks with calmer steps, like one
    Who goes with destiny.

And see, before him the great masts
    Tower with all their spars
Black on the dimness, soaring bold
    Among the mazy stars.

In stormy rushings through the air
    Wild scents the darkness filled,
And with a fierce forgetfulness
    His drinking nostril thrilled.

He hasted with quick feet, he hugged
    The wildness to his breast,
As one who goes the only way
    To set his heart at rest.

When morning glimmered, a great ship
    Dropt gliding down the shore.
John Winter coiled the anchor-ropes
    Among his mates once more.

*Laurence Binyon*

## THE GREENWICH PENSIONER

'Twas in the good ship *Rover*,
    I sailed the world all round,
And for three years and over
    I ne'er touched British ground.
At length in England landed,
    I left the roaring main,
Found all relations stranded,
    And went to sea again,
    And went to sea again.

That time bound straight for Portugal,
    Right fore and aft we bore,
But when we made Cape Ortegal,
    A gale blew off the shore.

She lay, so did it shock her,
  A log upon the main;
Till, saved from Davy's locker
  We put to sea again,
  We put to sea again.

Next sailing in a frigate
  I got my timber toe.
I never more shall jig it
  As once I used to do.
My leg was shot off fairly
  All by a ship of Spain;
But I could swab the galley,
  I went to sea again,
  I went to sea again.

And still I am enabled
  To bring up in the rear,
Although I'm quite disabled
  And lie in Greenwich tier.
There's schooners in the river,
  A-riding to the chain,
But I shall never, ever
  Put out to sea again,
  Put out to sea again.

*Anonymous*

### THE SAILOR'S CONSOLATION

ONE night came on a hurricane,
  The sea was mountains rolling,
When Barney Buntline turned his quid,
  And said to Billy Bowling:

"A strong nor'-wester's blowing, Bill;
  Hark! don't ye hear it roar, now?
Lord help 'em, how I pities all
  Unhappy folks on shore now!

"Foolhardy chaps who live in towns,
  What danger they are all in,
And now lie quaking in their beds,
  For fear the roof should fall in:
Poor creatures, how they envies us,
  And wishes, I've a notion,
For our good luck, in such a storm,
  To be upon the ocean!

"And as for them who're out all day,
  On business from their houses,
And late at night are coming home,
  To cheer the babes and spouses—
While you and I, Bill, on the deck,
  Are comfortably lying,
My eyes! what tiles and chimney-pots
  About their heads are flying!

"And very often have we heard
  How men are killed and undone,
By overturns of carriages,
  By thieves and fires in London;
We know what risks all landsmen run,
  From noblemen to tailors;
Then, Bill, let us thank Providence
  That you and I are sailors!"

*Charles Dibdin*

### DAVID GWYN

DAVID GWYN was a Welshman bold who pined a
    slave in the hulks of Spain,
Taken years since in some mad emprise with
    Francis Drake on the Spanish main.
Long in that cruel country he shared the captive's
    bitter and hapless lot;
Slowly the dead years passed and left him dream-
    ing still of the days that were not,
Of tiny Radnor, or stately Brecknock, or Cardi-
    gan's rain-swept heights may be,
Or green Caermarthen, or rich Glamorgan, or
    Pembroke sitting on either sea.
Sickening within his squalid prison, while still as
    the circling seasons came
The fierce sun beat on the brown Sierras, spring-
    tide and summer and autumn the same,
Almost hope failed the dauntless sailor, chained
    in an alien and hateful land,
Lonely and friendless, starved and buffeted, none
    to pity or understand,
Pining always and ageing yearly as slow Time
    whitened and bowed his head,
While longing and hate burned high and higher,
    as life sank lower and hope fell dead,
With brutes for his gaolers and fiends for his fellows,
    chained to him ceaselessly night and day,
Eleven autumns, eleven winters wasted their weari-
    some length away.
Then there awoke round his floating prison clang
    of hammers and bustle of men;

Shipwrights labouring late and early woke old
    thoughts in his heart again.
"Spain will lay waste your heretic island with fire
    and sword ere the winter be come,
And you and the rest of your felon crew shall row
    the galleys which sack your home."
The hot blood flushed to the prisoner's forehead,
    but never a word in reply said he,
Toiling obediently days and weeks till the great
    fleet sailed on the summer sea—
Splendid galleons towering skyward with gilded
    masts and with streamers brave,
Floating proudly to martial music over the blue
    Lusitanian wave,
Four great galleys leading the van, and in one
    midst the close-thronged benches sate
David Gwyn, a forgotten oarsman, nursing a burn-
    ing heart of hate.


So along the windless ocean slow the great
    Armada sped,
Two unclouded weeks of summer blazed the hot
    sun overhead.
Hourly from the high deck-pulpits preaching rose,
    and chant, and prayer,
And the cloying fumes of incense on the brisk
    Atlantic air;
Courtiers fine and sea-worn sailors jesting the
    slow hours away,
Silken sails and blazoned standards flapping idly
    day by day,

E

And within his high poop-turret, more than
  mortal to behold,
The High Admiral Medina lounging idly, clothed
  with gold.
Not a thought of peril touched them, not a dream
  of what might come,
Proudly sailing, sure of conquest, with the benison
  of Rome,
And far down among the oarsmen's benches,
  fainting, desperate,
David Gwyn, a patriot helpless with a burning
  heart of hate.

·    ·    ·    ·    ·

With the roaring Bay of Biscay louder winds and
  greyer skies,
And the galleons plunge and labour, and the
  rolling mountains rise;
Blacker loom the drifting storm-clouds, fiercer
  grow the wind and sea,
Far and wide the galleons scatter, driving, drifting
  helplessly.
Higher mount the thundering surges; tossed to
  heaven, or fathoms down,
Rear or plunge the cumbrous galleys while the
  helpless oarsmen drown.
Like a diver the *Diana* slides head first beneath
  the wave,
Not a soul of all her hundreds may her labouring
  consorts save.
Now to larboard, now to starboard, shattered,
  tossed from side to side,

Helpless rolls the great Armada, shorn of all its
    pomp and pride.
Down between those toppling ridges, groaning,
    straining in his place,
David Gwyn among the oarsmen sits with triumph
    in his face.

Then amid the roaring seas, when hope was gone
    and death was near,
And the hearts of all the Spanish sinking, failing
    them for fear,
Boldly to the haughty Captain, David Gwyn the
    oarsman went,
Veiling with a fearless frankness all the depth of
    his intent.
"Quick, Señor! the ship is sinking; like her
    consort will she be,
Buried soon with slaves and freemen, fathoms deep
    beneath the sea.
Give me leave and I will save her; I have fought
    the winds before,
Fought and conquered storms and foemen many
    a time on sea and shore."
And the haughty Captain, knowing David Gwyn
    a seaman bold,
Since upon the Spanish main the foemen sailed
    and fought of old,
Answered, turning to his prisoner: "Save the
    ship, and thou shalt gain
Freedom from thy life-long fetters, guerdon from
    the Lord of Spain."
Then from out the prisoner's eye there flashed a
    sudden gleam of flame,

And a light of secret triumph o'er his clouded
    visage came,
Thinking of his Cymric homestead and the fair
    years that were gone,
And his glory who should save her from the
    thraldom of the Don.
"I will save your ship," he answered; "trust me
    wholly, have no fear:
Pack the soldiers under hatches; leave the main
    deck free and clear."
Doubting much the Don consented; only, lest the
    slaves should rise,
By each oarsman sat a soldier, watching him with
    jealous eyes.
Little knew he of the cunning, secret signs, and
    watchwords born
Of long years of cruel fetters, stripes and hunger,
    spite and scorn.
Little thought he every prisoner as in misery he
    sate
Hid a dagger in his waistband, waiting for the call
    of Fate.

David Gwyn, the valiant seaman, long time
    battled with the main,
Till the furious storm-wind slackened and the
    ship was safe again.
Sudden then he gave the signal, raised his arm and
    bared his head.
Every oarsman rising swiftly stabbed his helpless
    warder dead,
Seized his arms, and, fired with conquest, mad
    with vengeance, like a flood

On the crowded 'tween-decks bursting, left the
    Spaniards in their blood.
David Gwyn was now the Captain, and the great
    ship all his own;
Well the slaves obeyed their comrade, thus to
    sudden greatness grown.
Straight for France the stout *Vasana* shaping,
    sudden on her lee
Don Diego in the *Royal*, foaming through the
    stricken sea,
Driven by full four hundred oarsmen, nigh the
    monstrous galley drew.
Then from out her thundering broadside swift the
    sudden lightning flew;
In among Gwyn's crowded seamen straight the
    hurtling missiles sped;
Nine strong sailors in a moment lay around their
    Captain dead.
David Gwyn, the dauntless Captain, turning to
    his comrades then—
"God has given you freedom; earn it: fear not;
    quit yourselves like men.
Lay the ship aboard the *Royal*: free your com-
    rades and be free."

The strong oarsmen bent, obedient, rowing swiftly,
    silently,
Till, as if in middle ocean striking on a hidden
    rock,
All the stout *Vasana's* timbers, quivering, reeling
    with the shock,
Straight on board the crowded *Royal* leapt that
    band of desperate men,

Freed the slaves, and left no Spaniard who might
tell the tale again;
And the sister galleys stately with fair winds sped
safely on,
Under David Gwyn, their Captain, and cast
anchor at Bayonne.
Then King Henry gave them largesse, and they
parted, every one
Free once more to his own country, and their evil
days were done.

*Sir Lewis Morris*

# FLIGHTS OF FANCY

## THE NIGHT BEFORE CHRISTMAS

'Twas the night before Christmas, when all
    through the house
Not a creature was stirring, not even a mouse;
The stockings were hung by the chimney with
    care,
In hopes that St Nicholas soon would be there;

The children were nestled all snug in their beds,
While visions of sugar-plums danced in their heads;
And Mamma in her kerchief, and I in my cap,
Had just settled our brains for a long winter's nap,

When out on the lawn there arose such a clatter,
I sprang from the bed to see what was the matter.
Away to the window I flew like a flash,
Tore open the shutters and threw up the sash.

The moon on the breast of the new-fallen snow
Gave the lustre of mid-day to objects below,
When, what to my wondering eyes should appear,
But a miniature sleigh, and eight tiny reindeer.

With a little old driver, so lively and quick,
I knew in a moment it must be St Nick.
More rapid than eagles his coursers they came,
And he whistled, and shouted, and called them
    by name:

"Now, *Dasher*! now, *Dancer*! now, *Prancer* and
    *Vixen*!
On, *Comet*! on, *Cupid*! on, *Donner* and *Blitzen*!
To the top of the porch! to the top of the wall!
Now dash away! dash away! dash away all!"

As dry leaves that before the wild hurricane fly,
When they meet with an obstacle, mount to the
    sky,
So up to the house-top the coursers they flew,
With the sleigh full of Toys, and St Nicholas too.

And then, in a twinkling, I heard on the roof
The prancing and pawing of each little hoof.
As I drew in my head, and was turning around,
Down the chimney St Nicholas came with a bound.

He was dressed all in fur, from his head to his foot,
And his clothes were all tarnished with ashes and
    soot;
A bundle of Toys he had flung on his back,
And he looked like a pedlar just opening his pack.

His eyes—how they twinkled! his dimples how
    merry!
His cheeks were like roses, his nose like a cherry!
His droll little mouth was drawn up like a bow,
And the beard of his chin was as white as the
    snow;

The stump of a pipe he held tight in his teeth,
And the smoke it encircled his head like a wreath;
He had a broad face and a little round belly,
That shook, when he laughed, like a bowlful of
    jelly.

He was chubby and plump, a right jolly old elf,
And I laughed when I saw him, in spite of myself;
A wink of his eye and a twist of his head
Soon gave me to know I had nothing to dread.

He spoke not a word, but went straight to his
    work,
And filled all the stockings; then turned with a
    jerk,
And laying his finger aside of his nose,
And giving a nod, up the chimney he rose;

He sprang to his sleigh, to his team gave a whistle,
And away they all flew like the down of a thistle.
But I heard him exclaim, ere he drove out of sight,
"*Happy Christmas to all and to all a good-night!*"

Clement C. Moore

## THE FAIRY SHOEMAKER

LITTLE Cowboy, what have you heard,
  Up on the lonely rath's green mound?
Only the plaintive yellow bird
  Sighing in sultry fields around,
Chary, chary, chary, chee-ee!
Only the grasshopper and the bee?—
     "Tip-tap, rip-rap,
      Tick-a-tack too!
    Scarlet leather, sewn together,
     This will make a shoe.

Left, right, pull it tight;
   Summer days are warm;
Underground in winter,
   Laughing at the storm!"
Lay your ear close to the hill.
   Do you not catch the tiny clamour—
   Busy-click of an elfin hammer,
Voice of the Leprechaun singing shrill
   As he merrily plies his trade?
      He's a span
      And a quarter in height.
Get him in sight, hold him tight,
      And you're a made
      Man!


You watch your cattle the summer day,
Sup on potatoes, sleep in the hay;
   How would you like to roll in your carriage,
   Look for a duchess's daughter in marriage?
Seize the Shoemaker—then you may!
      "Big boots a-hunting
      Sandals in the hall,
      White for a wedding-feast,
      Pink for a ball.
      This way, that way
      So we make a shoe;
      Getting rich every stitch,
      Tick-tack-too!"
Nine-and-ninety treasure-crocks
   This keen miser-fairy hath,
Hid in mountains, woods, and rocks,
   Ruin and round-tow'r, cave and rath,

And where the cormorants build;
        From times of old
        Guarded by him;
        Each of them fill'd
        Full to the brim
            With gold!


I caught him at work one day, myself,
    In the castle-ditch where foxglove grows,
A wrinkled, wizen'd, and bearded elf,
    Spectacles stuck on his pointed nose,
    Silver buckles to his hose,
        Leather apron—shoe in his lap—
            "Rip-rap, tip-tap,
            Tack-tack-too!
        (A grasshopper on my cap!
            Away the moth flew!)
        Buskins for a fairy prince,
            Brogues for his son,
        Pay me well, pay me well
            When the job is done!"
The rogue was mine, beyond a doubt.
    I stared at him; he stared at me;
    "Servant, Sir!" "Humph!" says he,
And pull'd a snuff-box out.
He took a long pinch, look'd better pleased,
    The queer little Leprechaun;
Offer'd the box with a whimsical grace,—
Pouf! he flung the dust in my face,
        And, while I sneezed,
            Was gone!

                            *William Allingham*

### ROBIN GOODFELLOW

From Oberon, in fairyland,
  The king of ghosts and shadows there,
Mad Robin I, at his command,
  Am sent to view the night-sports here.
        What revel rout
        Is kept about,
    In every corner where I go,
      I will o'ersee, and merry be,
    And make good sport, with ho, ho, ho!

More swift than lightning can I fly
  About this aery welkin soon,
And, in a minute's space, descry
  Each thing that's done below the moon.
        There's not a hag
        Or ghost shall wag,
    Or cry, 'ware goblins! where I go;
      But Robin I their feats will spy,
    And send them home, with ho, ho, ho!

Whene'er such wanderers I meet,
  As from their night-sports they trudge
    home,
With counterfeiting voice I greet,
  And call them on with me to roam:
        Through woods, through lakes,
        Through bogs, through brakes;
    Or else, unseen, with them I go,
      All in the nick to play some trick,
    And frolic it, with ho, ho, ho!

Sometimes I meet them like a man,
　Sometimes an ox, sometimes a hound;
And to a horse I turn me can,
　To trip and trot about them round.
　　　　But if to ride
　　　　My back they stride,
　More swift than wind away I go,
　　O'er hedge and lands, through pools and ponds,
　I hurry, laughing, ho, ho, ho!

When lads and lasses merry be,
　With possets and with junkets fine,
Unseen of all the company,
　I eat their cakes and sip their wine!
　　　　And, to make sport,
　　　　I puff and snort;
　And out the candles I do blow:
　　The maids I kiss; they shriek—Who's this?
　I answer naught but ho, ho, ho!

Yet now and then, the maids to please,
　At midnight I card up their wool;
And, while they sleep and take their ease,
　With wheel to threads their flax I pull.
　　　　I grind at mill
　　　　Their malt up still;
　I dress their hemp; I spin their tow;
　　If any 'wake, and would me take,
　I wend me, laughing, ho, ho, ho!

When any need to borrow aught,
　We lend them what they do require;
And, for the use demand we nought,
　Our own is all we do desire.

If to repay
They do delay,
Abroad amongst them then I go,
    And night by night, I them affright
    With pinchings, dreams, and ho, ho, ho!


When lazy queans have nought to do,
    But study how to cog and lye,
To make debate and mischief too,
    'Twixt one another secretly,
            I mark their gloze,
            And it disclose
    To them whom they have wrongèd so;
        When I have done, I get me gone,
        And leave them scolding, ho, ho, ho!


When men do traps and engines set
    In loop-holes where the vermin creep,
Who from their folds and houses get
    Their ducks and geese, and lambs and sheep,
            I spy the gin,
            And enter in,
    And seem a vermin taken so,
        But when they there approach me near,
        I leap out laughing, ho, ho, ho!


By wells and rills, in meadows green,
    We nightly dance our heyday guise,
And to our fairy king and queen
    We chant our moonlight minstrelsies.
            When larks 'gin sing,
            Away we fling,

And babes new-born steal as we go,
    And elf in bed we leave instead,
And wend us laughing, ho, ho, ho!

From hag-bred Merlin's time have I
    Thus nightly revelled to and fro;
And for my pranks men call me by
    The name of Robin Good-fellôw.
        Fiends, ghosts, and sprites,
        Who haunt the nights,
    The hags and goblins do me know;
        And beldames old my feats have told,
    So, vale, vale; ho, ho, ho!

*Anonymous*

## THE BALLAD OF THE OYSTERMAN

It was a tall young oysterman lived by the river-
    side,
His shop was just upon the bank, his boat was on
    the tide;
The daughter of a fisherman, that was so straight
    and slim,
Lived over on the other bank, right opposite to
    him.

It was the pensive oysterman that saw a lovely
    maid,
Upon a moonlight evening, a-sitting in the
    shade;

He saw her wave a handkerchief, as much as if
 to say,
"I'm wide awake, young oysterman, and all the
 folks away."

Then up arose the oysterman, and to himself said
 he,
"I guess I'll leave the skiff at home, for fear
 that folks should see;
I read it in the story-book, that, for to kiss his dear,
Leander swam the Hellespont—and I will swim
 this here."

And he has leaped into the waves, and crossed the
 shining stream,
And he has clambered up the bank, all in the
 moonlight gleam;
Oh, there are kisses sweet as dew, and words as
 soft as rain—
But they have heard her father's step, and in he
 leaps again!

Out spoke the ancient fisherman: "Oh, what was
 that, my daughter?"
"'Twas nothing but a pebble, sir, I threw into the
 water."
"And what is that, pray tell me, love, that
 paddles off so fast?"
"It's nothing but a porpoise, sir, that's been
 a-swimming past."

Out spoke the ancient fisherman: "Now, bring
 me my harpoon!
I'll get into my fishing-boat, and fix the fellow
 soon."

Down fell that pretty innocent, as falls a snow-
    white lamb;
Her hair drooped round her pallid cheeks, like
    seaweed on a clam.

Alas for those two loving ones! she waked not
    from her swound,
And he was taken with a cramp, and in the waves
    was drowned;
But Fate has metamorphosed them, in pity of
    their woe,
And now they keep an oyster-shop for mermaids
    down below.

*Oliver Wendell Holmes*

### THE CLERK OF THE WEATHER

THE Clerk of the Weather's a wonderful wizard
At brewing a tempest, a hailstorm, or blizzard,
Or thunder and lightning, or cloudburst, or squall,
But at making bright sunshine he's no good at all.

He lives in Hyde Park in a cave near the centre,
Which no one more human than wizards can enter;
His magical spells keep it hidden from sight;
Oh! he's clever at spells, is this weather-wise
    wight.

And in it he keeps a huge cauldron of copper:
(What gallons and gallons it holds! what a
    whopper!)

F

He fills it each night from the main overhead,
Then he makes up the fire, ere he limps off to bed.

Next morning, quite early, it's just about boiling,
And steam-clouds are rising and writhing and
    coiling;
A pass from his wand, another, and then
All the good folk above say, "It's raining again!"

But when he gets up feeling savage or grumpy,
A bit out-of-sorts, or unpleasant, or humpy,
He works off his temper, his rage, and his spite,
Just by giving the people of London a fright.

"Ye vipers and lizards, snails, beetles, and spiders,
All hoppers, and jumpers, and creepers, and
    gliders,
Ye vultures, hyenas, and scorpions, and bats,
And ye crocodiles, vampires, and brindle-furred
    cats!

"Come here to my aid, bring your arts and your
    magic,
I ask you, command you, to brew something
    tragic,
A fog, a pea-souper, or thunder and hail,
Or the blast of the storm and the rage of the gale."

He stirs up the coals, as he mutters and mumbles,
And round him come sounds and mysterious
    rumbles
And rustles, and everywhere eyes sparkle bright,
Like the stars in the sky on a cold frosty night.

And ghastly blue flames rise and flutter and
    flicker,
While each of the crew casts a spell on the liquor:
Then follows a snowstorm, and thunder, and fog,
And the weather's too awful to turn out a dog.

But sometimes he gets to the end of his tether;
He tires himself out, does the Clerk of the Weather;
He drops off to sleep in a heap on the floor,
And he stays there a day or a week, or p'raps more.

It's then that the mornings are sunny and jolly,
But don't trust them always; a mac or a brolly
Is easy to carry; the wicked old Clerk
Loves to wake up and drench you: he thinks it's
    a lark.

Oh! the Clerk of the Weather's a wonderful
    wizard
At brewing a tempest, a hailstorm, or blizzard,
Or thunder and lightning, or cloudburst, or squall;
But at keeping fine weather he's no good at all.

*P. E. Herrick*

WILLOW THE KING

Willow the King is a monarch grand:
Three in a row his courtiers stand;
Every day, when the sun shines bright,
The walls of his palace are painted white,

And all the company bow their backs
To the King with his collar of cobbler's wax.
        So ho! so ho! may the courtiers sing:
        Honour and life to Willow the King!


Willow, King Willow, thy guard hold tight!
Trouble is coming before the night:
Hopping and galloping, short and strong,
Comes the Leathery Duke along;
And down the palaces tumble fast
When once the Leathery Duke gets past.
        So ho! so ho! may the courtiers sing:
        Honour and life to Willow the King!


"Who is this," King Willow he swore,
"Hops like that to a gentleman's door?
Who's afraid of a Duke like him?
Fiddlededee!" says the monarch slim:
"What do you say, my courtiers three?"
And the courtiers all said "Fiddlededee!"
        So ho! so ho! may the courtiers sing:
        Honour and life to Willow the King!


Willow the King stood forward bold
Three good feet from his castle-hold;
Willow the King stepped back so light,
Skirmished gay to the left and right;
But the Duke rushed by with a leap and a
    fling—
"Bless my soul!" says Willow the King.
        So ho! so ho! may the courtiers sing:
        Honour and life to Willow the King!

Crash the palaces, sad to see;
Crash and tumble the courtiers three!
Each one lays, in his fear and dread,
Down on the grass his respected head;
Each one kicks, as he downward goes,
Up in the air his respected toes.
> So ho! so ho! may the courtiers sing:
> Honour and life to Willow the King!

But the Leathery Duke he jumped so high,
Jumped till he almost touched the sky:
"A fig for King Willow!" he boasting said;
"Carry this gentleman off to bed!"
So they carried him off with the courtiers three,
And put him to bed in the green-baize tree.
> So ho! so ho! may the courtiers sing:
> Honour and life to Willow the King!

"What of the Duke?" you ask anon:
"Where has his Leathery Highness gone?"
Oh, he is filled with air inside!
Either it's air, or else it's pride—
And he swells and swells as light as a drum,
And they kick him about till Christmas come.
> So ho! so ho! may his courtiers sing:
> Honour and life to Willow the King!

*E. E. Bowen*

# VARIOUS ADVENTURES

## SADDLE TO RAGS

THIS story I'm going to sing,
    I hope it will give you content,
Concerning a silly old man
    That was going to pay his rent.

As he was a-riding along,
    Along all on the highway,
A gentleman-thief overtook him,
    And thus unto him he did say:

"O well overtaken, old man,
    O well overtaken," said he:
"Thank you kindly, sir," says the old man,
    "If you be for my company."

"How far are you going this way?"
    It made the old man to smile;
"To tell you the truth, kind sir,
    I'm just a-going twa mile.

"I am but a silly old man,
    Who farms a piece of ground;
My half-year rent, kind sir,
    Just comes to forty pound.

"But my landlord's not been at hame—
    I've not seen him twelve month or more;
It makes my rent to be large,
    I've just to pay him fourscore."

"You should not have told anybody,
  For thieves they are ganging many;
If they were to light upon you
  They would rob you of every penny."

"O! never mind," says the old man,
  "Thieves I fear on no side;
My money is safe in my bags,
  In the saddle on which I ride."

As they were a-riding along,
  And riding a-down a ghyll,
The thief pulled out a pistòl,
  And bade the old man stand still.

The old man was crafty and false,
  As in this world are many;
He flung his old saddle o'er t' hedge,
  And said, "Fetch it, if thou'lt have any."

The thief got off his horse,
  With courage stout and bold,
To search this old man's bags,
  And gave him his horse to hold.

The old man put foot in stirrup,
  And he got on astride;
He set the thief's horse in a gallop—
  You need not bid th' old man ride!

"O stay! O stay!" says the thief,
  "And thou half my share shalt have."
"Nay, marry, not I," quoth the old man,
  "For once I've bitten a knave!"

This thief he was not content,
    He thought there *must* be bags,
So he up with his rusty sword,
    And chopped the old saddle to rags.

The old man galloped and rode,
    Until he was almost spent,
Till he came to his landlord's house,
    And he paid him his whole year's rent.

He opened this rogue's portmantle,
    It was glorious for to behold;
There was five hundred pound in money,
    And other five hundred in gold.

*Anonymous*


### THE PRIEST AND THE MULBERRY-TREE

DID you hear of the curate who mounted his mare,
And merrily trotted along to the fair?
Of creature more tractable none ever heard:
In the height of her speed she would stop at a word;
But again with a word, when the curate said,
    "Hey,"
She put forth her mettle and galloped away.

As near to the gates of the city he rode,
While the sun of September all brilliantly glowed,
The good priest discovered, with eyes of desire,
A mulberry-tree in a hedge of wild-briar;
On boughs long and lofty, in many a green shoot,
Hung, large, black, and glossy, the beautiful fruit.

The curate was hungry, and thirsty to boot;
He shrank from the thorns, though he longed for
    the fruit;
With a word he arrested his courser's keen speed,
And he stood up erect on the back of his steed;
On the saddle he stood while the creature stood
    still,
And he gathered the fruit till he took his good fill.

"Sure never," he thought, "was a creature so rare,
So docile, so true, as my excellent mare;
Lo, here, how I stand," (and he gazed all around),
"As safe and as steady as if on the ground;
Yet how had it been, if some traveller this way,
Had, dreaming no mischief, but chanced to cry
    'Hey'?"

He stood with his head in the mulberry-tree,
And he spoke out aloud in his fond reverie;
At the sound of the word the good mare made a
    push,
And down went the priest in the wild-briar bush.
He remembered too late, on his thorny green bed,
Much that well may be thought, cannot wisely be
    said.

*T. L. Peacock*

## THE ENCHANTED SHIRT

THE King was sick.  His cheek was red
  And his eye was clear and bright;
He ate and drank with kingly zest,
  And peacefully snored at night.

But he said he was sick, and a King should know,
    And doctors came by the score.
They did not cure him.   He cut off their heads
    And sent to the schools for more.

At last two famous doctors came,
    And one was as poor as a rat,
He had passed his life in studious toil,
    And never found time to grow fat.

The other had never looked in a book;
    His patients gave him no trouble,
If they recovered they paid him well,
    If they died their heirs paid double.

Together they looked at the royal tongue,
    As the King on his couch reclined;
In succession they thumped his august chest,
    But no trace of disease could find.

The old sage said, "You're as sound as a nut."
    "Hang him up!" roared the King in a gale,
In a ten-knot gale of royal rage;
    The other leech grew a shade pale;

But he pensively rubbed his sagacious nose,
    And thus his prescription ran—
*The King will be well if he sleeps one night*
    *In the Shirt of a Happy Man.*

Wide o'er the realm the couriers rode,
    And fast their horses ran,
And many they saw, and to many they spoke,
    But they found no Happy Man.

They found poor men who would fain be rich,
    And rich who thought they were poor;
And men who twisted their waists in stays,
    And women that short-hose wore.

They saw two men by the roadside sit,
    And both bemoaned their lot;
For one had buried his wife, he said,
    And the other one had not.

At last they came to a village gate,
    A beggar lay whistling there;
He whistled and sang and laughed and rolled
    On the grass in the soft June air.

The weary couriers paused and looked
    At the scamp so blithe and gay;
And one of them said, "Heaven save you, friend,
    You seem to be happy to-day."

"O yes, fair Sirs," the rascal laughed,
    And his voice rang free and glad,
"An idle man has so much to do
    That he never has time to be sad."

"This is our man," the courier said,
    "Our luck has led us aright.
I will give you a hundred ducats, friend,
    For the loan of your shirt to-night."

The merry blackguard lay back on the grass,
    And laughed till his face was black;
"I would do it, God wot," and he roared with
        the fun,
    "But I haven't a shirt to my back."

Each day to the King the reports came in
    Of his unsuccessful spies,
And the sad panorama of human woes
    Passed daily under his eyes.

And he grew ashamed of his useless life,
    And his maladies hatched in gloom;
He opened his windows and let in the air
    Of the free heaven into his room.

And out he went in the world and toiled
    In his own appointed way;
And the people blessed him, the land was glad,
    And the King was well and gay.

*John Hay*

### BISHOP HATTO

THE summer and autumn had been so wet
That in winter the corn was growing yet;
'Twas a piteous sight to see all around
The grain lie rotting on the ground.

Every day the starving poor
Crowded around Bishop Hatto's door,
For he had a plentiful last year's store,
And all the neighbourhood could tell,
His granaries were furnished well.

At last Bishop Hatto appointed a day
To quiet the poor without delay;

He bade them to his great barn repair,
And they should have food for the winter there.


Rejoiced at such tidings good to hear,
The poor folk flocked from far and near,
The great barn was full as it could hold
Of women and children, and young and old.


Then, when he saw it could hold no more,
Bishop Hatto he made fast the door;
And while for mercy on Christ they call,
He set fire to the barn, and burnt them all.


"I' faith, 'tis an excellent bonfire!" quoth he,
"And the country is greatly obliged to me
For ridding it, in these times forlorn,
Of rats, that only consume the corn!"


So then to his palace returnèd he,
And he sat down to supper right merrily,
And he slept that night like an innocent man;
But Bishop Hatto never slept again.


In the morning, when he entered the hall,
Where his picture hung against the wall,
A sweat like death all over him came,
For the rats had eaten it out of the frame.


As he look'd there came a man from his farm,
And he had a countenance white with alarm;
"My lord, I opened your granaries this morn,
And the rats had eaten all your corn."

Another came running presently,
And he was pale as pale could be.
"Fly! my Lord Bishop, fly!" quoth he,
"Ten thousand rats are coming this way—
The Lord forgive you for yesterday!"

"I'll go to my tower on the Rhine," replied he;
" 'Tis the safest place in Germany;
The walls are high, and the shores are steep,
And the stream is strong, and the water deep."

Bishop Hatto fearfully hastened away,
And he crossed the Rhine without delay,
And reached his tower, and barred with care
All the windows, doors, and loopholes there.

He laid him down and closed his eyes,
But soon a scream made him arise;
He started, and saw two eyes of flame
On his pillow from whence the screaming came.

He listened and looked; it was only the cat;
But the Bishop he grew more fearful for that,
For she sat screaming, mad with fear,
At the army of Rats, that was drawing near.

For they have swum over the river so deep,
And they have climbed the shore so steep,
And now by thousands up they crawl
To the holes and windows in the wall.

Down on his knees the Bishop fell,
And faster and faster his beads did he tell,
As louder and louder, drawing near
The saw of their teeth without he could hear.

And in at the windows, and in at the door,
And through the walls by thousands they pour,
And down through the ceiling, and up through
    the floor,
From the right and the left, from behind and
    before,
From within and without, from above and below—
And all at once to the Bishop they go.

They have whetted their teeth against the stones,
And now they pick the Bishop's bones;
They gnawed the flesh from every limb,
For they were sent to do judgment on him.

*Robert Southey*


## KING JOHN AND THE ABBOT OF CANTERBURY

AN ancient story I'll tell you anon
Of a notable prince that was called King John;
And he rulèd England with main and with might,
For he did great wrong and maintained little right.

And I'll tell you a story, a story so merry,
Concerning the Abbot of Canterbury;
How for his house-keeping, and high renown,
They rode post for him to fair London town.

An hundred men, the king did hear say,
The abbot kept in his house every day;
And fifty gold chains, without any doubt,
In velvet coats waited the abbot about.

"How now, father abbot, I hear it of thee,
Thou keepest a far better house than me,
And for thy house-keeping and high renown,
I fear thou work'st treason against my crown."

"My liege," quo' the abbot, "I would it were known
I never spend nothing but what is my own;
And I trust your grace will do me no dere
For spending of my own true-gotten gear."

"Yes, yes, father abbot, thy fault it is high,
And now for the same thou needest must die;
For except thou canst answer me questions three,
Thy head shall be smitten from thy bodie.

"And first," quo' the king, "when I'm in this stead,
With my crown of gold so fair on my head,
Among all my liege-men so noble of birth,
Thou must tell me to one penny what I am worth.

"Secondly, tell me, without any doubt,
How soon I may ride the whole world about.
And at the third question thou must not shrink,
But tell me here truly what I do think."

"O, these are hard questions for my shallow wit,
Nor I cannot answer your grace as yet:
But if you will give me but three weeks' space,
I'll do my endeavour to answer your grace."

"Now three weeks' space to thee will I give,
And that is the longest thou hast to live;
For if thou dost not answer my questions three,
Thy lands and thy livings are forfeit to me."

Away rode the abbot all sad at that word,
And he rode to Cambridge and Oxenford;
But never a doctor there was so wise
That could with his learning an answer devise.

Then home rode the abbot of comfort so cold,
And he met his shepherd a-going to fold:
"How now, my lord abbot, you are welcome
    home;
What news do you bring us from good King
    John?"

"Sad news, sad news, shepherd, I must give,
That I have but three days more to live;
For if I do not answer him questions three,
My head will be smitten from my bodie.

"The first is to tell him, there in that stead,
With his crown of gold so fair on his head,
Among all his liege-men so noble of birth,
To within one penny of what he is worth.

"The second, to tell him, without any doubt,
How soon he may ride this whole world about;
And at the third question I must not shrink,
To tell him there truly what he does think."

"Now cheer up, sire abbot! Did you never hear
    yet,
That a fool he may learn a wise man wit?
Lend me horse, and serving-men, and your apparel,
And I'll ride to London to answer your quarrel.

G

"Nay, frown not, if it hath been told unto me,
I am like your lordship as ever may be:
And if you will but lend me your gown,
There is none shall know us at fair London town."

"Now horses and serving-men thou shalt have,
With sumptuous array most gallant and brave,
With crozier, and mitre, and rochet, and cope,
Fit to appear 'fore our father the Pope."

"Now welcome, sire abbot," the king he did say,
" 'Tis well thou'rt come back to keep thy day;
For and if thou canst answer my questions three,
Thy life and thy living both savèd shall be.

"And first, when thou seest me here in this stead,
With my crown of gold so fair on my head,
Among all my liege-men so noble of birth,
Tell me to one penny what I am worth."

"For thirty pence our Saviour was sold
Among the false Jews, as I have been told,
And twenty-nine is the worth of thee,
For I think thou'rt one penny worser than He."

The king he laughed and swore by St Bittel,
"I did not think I had been worth so little!
—Now secondly tell me, without any doubt,
How soon I may ride this whole world about."

"You must rise with the sun, and ride with the
        same,
Until the next morning he riseth again;
And then your grace need not make any doubt
But in twenty-four hours you'll ride it about."

The king he laughed, and swore by St John,
"I did not think I could do it so soon!
—Now from the third question thou must not
    shrink,
But tell me here truly what I do think."

"Yea, that shall I do, and make your grace
    merry;
You think I'm the abbot of Canterbury;
But I'm his poor shepherd, as plain you may see,
That am come to beg pardon for him and for me."

The king he laughed, and swore by the Mass,
"I'll make thee lord abbot this day in his place!"
"Now nay, my liege, be not in such speed,
For alack! I can neither write nor read."

"Four nobles a week, then, I will give thee,
For this merry jest thou hast shown unto me;
And tell the old abbot, when thou comest home,
Thou hast brought him a pardon from good King
    John."

*Anonymous*

### HEATHER ALE

FROM the bonny bells of heather
    They brewed a drink long-syne,
Was sweeter far than honey,
    Was stronger far than wine.

They brewed it and they drank it,
    And lay in a blessèd swound
For days and days together
    In their dwellings underground.


There rose a king in Scotland,
    A fell man to his foes,
He smote the Picts in battle,
    He hunted them like roes.
Over miles of the red mountain
    He hunted as they fled,
And strewed the dwarfish bodies
    Of the dying and the dead.


Summer came in the country,
    Red was the heather-bell;
But the manner of the brewing
    Was none alive to tell.
In graves that were like children's
    On many a mountain head,
The Brewsters of the Heather
    Lay numbered with the dead.


The king in the red moorland
    Rode on a summer's day;
And the bees hummed, and the curlews
    Cried beside the way.
The king rode, and was angry,
    Black was his brow and pale,
To rule in a land of heather
    And lack the Heather Ale.

It fortuned that his vassals,
   Riding free on the heath,
Came on a stone that was fallen
   And vermin hid beneath.
Rudely plucked from their hiding,
   Never a word they spoke:
A son and his agèd father—
   Last of the dwarfish folk.


The king sat high on his charger,
   He looked on the little men;
And the dwarfish and swarthy couple
   Looked at the king again.
Down by the shore he had them;
   And there on the giddy brink—
"I will give you life, ye vermin,
   For the secret of the drink."


There stood the son and father
   And they looked high and low;
The heather was red around them,
   The sea rumbled below.
And up and spoke the father,
   Shrill was his voice to hear:
"I have a word in private,
   A word for the royal ear.


"Life is dear to the agèd,
   And honour a little thing;
I would gladly sell the secret,"
   Quoth the Pict to the king.

His voice was small as a sparrow's,
    And shrill and wonderful clear;
"I would gladly sell my secret,
    Only my son I fear.

"For life is a little matter
    And death is nought to the young;
And I dare not sell my honour
    Under the eye of my son.
Take him, O king, and bind him,
    And cast him far in the deep;
And it's I will tell the secret
    That I have sworn to keep."

They took the son and bound him,
    Neck and heels in a thong,
And a lad took him and swung him,
    And flung him far and strong,
And the sea swallowed his body,
    Like that of a child of ten;
And there on the cliff stood the father,
    Last of the dwarfish men.

"True was the word I told you:
    Only my son I feared;
For I doubt the sapling courage
    That goes without the beard.
But now in vain is the torture,
    Fire shall never avail:
Here dies in my bosom
    The secret of Heather Ale."

                                *Robert Louis Stevenson*

### ROBIN HOOD AND THE THREE SQUIRES

THERE are twelve months in all the year,
    As I hear many men say,
But the merriest month in all the year
    Is the merry month of May.

Now Robin Hood is to Nottingham gone,
    *With a link a down and a day,*
And there he met a silly old woman,
    Was weeping on the way.

"What news, what news, thou silly old woman?
    What news hast thou for me?"
Said she, "There's three squires in Nottingham
        town
    To-day is condemned to die."

"Oh what have they done?" said Robin Hood,
    "I pray thee tell to me."
"It's for slaying of the King's fallow deer,
    Bearing their long-bows with thee."

Now Robin Hood is to Nottingham gone,
    *With a link a down and a day,*
And there he met with a silly old palmer,
    Was walking along the highway.

"What news, what news, thou silly old man?
    What news, I do thee pray?"
Said he, "Three squires in Nottingham town
    Are condemned to die this day."

"Come, change thy apparel with me, old man,
    Come, change thy apparel for mine;
Here is forty shillings in good silver—
    Go drink it in beer or wine."

"O thine apparel is good," he said,
    "And mine is ragged and torn;
Wherever you go, wherever you ride,
    Laugh ne'er an old man to scorn."

"Come, change thy apparel with me, old churl,
    Come, change thy apparel with mine;
Here are twenty pieces of good broad gold,
    Go feast thy brethren with wine."

Then he put on the old man's hat,
    It stood full high on the crown;
"The first bold bargain that I come at,
    It shall make thee come down."

Then he put on the old man's cloak,
    Was patched black, blue, and red;
He thought no shame all the day long
    To wear the bags of bread.

Then he put on the old man's breeks,
    Was patched from side to side.
"By the truth of my body," bold Robin can say,
    "This man loved little pride."

Then he put on the old man's hose,
    Were patched from knee to wrist;
"By the truth of my body," said bold Robin Hood,
    "I'd laugh if I had any list."

Then he put on the old man's shoes,
  Were patched both beneath and aboon;
Then Robin Hood swore a solemn oath,
  "It's good habit that makes a man."

Now Robin Hood is to Nottingham gone,
  *With a link a down and a down,*
And there he met with the proud sheriff,
  Was walking along the town.

"O save, O save, O sheriff," he said,
  "O save, and you may see;
And what will you give to a silly old man
  To-day will your hangman be?"

"Some suits, some suits," the sheriff he said,
  "Some suits I'll give to thee;
Some suits, some suits, and pence thirteen
  To-day's a hangman's fee."

Then Robin he turns him round about,
  And jumps from stock to stone;
"By the truth of my body," the sheriff he said,
  "That's well jumpt, thou nimble old man."

"I was ne'er a hangman in all my life,
  Nor yet intend to trade;
But curst be he," said bold Robin,
  "That first a hangman was made.

"I've a bag for meal, and a bag for malt,
  And a bag for barley and corn;
A bag for bread, and a bag for beef,
  And a bag for my little small horn.

"I have a horn in my pocket,
    I got it from Robin Hood;
And still when I set it to my mouth,
    For thee it blows little good."


"O wind thy horn, thou proud fellow,
    Of thee I have no doubt;
I wish that thou give such a blast
    Till both thine eyes fall out."


The first loud blast that he did blow,
    He blew both loud and shrill;
A hundred and fifty of Robin Hood's men
    Came riding over the hill.


The next loud blast that he did give,
    He blew both loud and amain;
And quickly sixty of Robin Hood's men
    Came shining over the plain.


"O who are you?" the sheriff he said,
    "Come tripping over the lee?"
"They're my attendants," brave Robin did
        say,
    "They'll pay a visit to thee."


They took the gallows from the slack,
    They set it in the glen;
They hanged the proud sheriff on that,
    Released their own three men.

                                *Anonymous*

# A MEDLEY OF MIRTH

## CLEAN CLARA

WHAT! not know our Clean Clara?
Why, the hot folks in Sahara,
And the cold Esquimaux,
Our little Clara know!
Clean Clara, the Poet sings,
Cleaned a hundred thousand things!

She cleaned the keys of the harpsichord,
She cleaned the hilt of the family sword,
She cleaned my lady, she cleaned my lord;
All the pictures in their frames,
Knights with daggers, and stomachered dames—
Cecils, Godfreys, Montforts, Graemes,
Winifreds—all those nice old names!

She cleaned the works of the eight-day clock,
She cleaned the spring of a secret lock,
She cleaned the mirror, she cleaned the cupboard;
All the books she india-rubbered!

She cleaned the Dutch tiles in the place,
She cleaned some very old-fashioned lace;
The Countess of Miniver came to her,,
"Pray, my dear, will you clean my fur?"
All her cleanings were admirable;
To count your teeth you will be able,
If you look in the walnut table!

She cleaned the tent-stitch and the sampler;
She cleaned the tapestry, which was ampler;
Joseph going down into the pit,
And the Shunammite woman with a boy in
    a fit.


You saw the reapers, *not* in the distance,
And Elisha coming to the child's assistance,
With the house on the wall that was built for the
    prophet,
The chair, the bed, and the bolster of it;


The eyebrows all had a twirl reflective,
Just like an eel: to spare invective,
There was plenty of colour, but no perspective.
However, Clara cleaned it all,
With a curious lamp, that hangs in the hall;
She cleaned the drops of the chandeliers,
Madam in mittens was moved to tears!


She cleaned the cage of the cockatoo,
The oldest bird that ever grew;
I should say a thousand years old would
    do—
I'm sure he looked it; but nobody knew;
She cleaned the china, she cleaned the delf,
She cleaned the baby, she cleaned herself!


To-morrow morning she means to try
To clean the cobwebs from the sky;
Some people say the girl will rue it,
But my belief is she will do it.

So I've made up my mind to be there to see:
There's a beautiful place in the walnut-tree;
The bough is as firm as the solid rock;
She brings out her broom at six o'clock.

*W. B. Rands*


SIR SEPTIMUS

Sir Septimus Meek
    Was a great baronet;
But his voice had a squeak,
    And he used to forget
What he said, so he'd speak
It all over again, to make sure.
But Sir Septimus couldn't endure
To be told (though with greatest respect)
"You are old, sir, and mustn't expect
    Every time to remember
    The Fifth of November;
  Though of course it is shocking
  Not to hang up your stocking
On the twenty-fourth night of December."

Sir Septimus Meek
    Was a great baronet;
But his voice had a squeak,
    And he used to forget
All the days of the week,
And especially Saturday night—-
It was bath-night on Saturday night.

But they told him (with greatest respect)
"Though you're old, sir, you mustn't expect
 To escape a good wetting
 Through merely forgetting.
So we'll give you a rub, sir,
And then a good scrub, sir,
And it's no use your fuming and fretting."


 Sir Septimus Meek
  Was a great baronet;
 But his voice had a squeak,
  And he used to forget
 How to play hide-and-seek.
He mislaid all his boots, he'd so many,
And would toddle around without any;
So they told him (with greatest respect)
You are old, sir, and mustn't expect
 To defy altogether
 This inclement weather.
Let us find you some bootsies
To put on your tootsies;
Then your knees won't go knocking together.


 Sir Septimus Meek
  Was a great baronet;
 And his relatives speak
  Of the old fellow yet:
 How his voice had a squeak,
And he used to forget what he said,
And couldn't keep dates in his head.
But we're told (with the greatest respect)
He was old, so he couldn't expect

Every time to remember
The Fifth of November,
Though of course it was shocking
Not to hang up his stocking
On the twenty-fourth night of December.

*A. E. M. Bayliss*

## PEGGY LEG

THERE once was a one-leggèd man who was brave
    as the lions in the zoo.
He lived long ago, you may guess, since he fought
    upon the field of Waterloo.
He marched to the fray on the two flattest feet
    you could ever wish to find.
They wheeled him away at the end of the day
    leaving one of 'em behind.

They gave him a nice wooden leg, and they made
    him the drummer in a band;
And he banged on his drum every day of his life
    and begged for coppers in the Strand.
"Oh, the loss of a foot or a leg needn't wholly
    be deplored," said he.
"A half-pair of trousers and only one boot is a
    great economy!"

He grew very old and nearly as wise as a hermit
    in a cave;
And he never grew tired of remarking the fact
    that he'd one foot in the grave.

But the end came at last, as the end always must,
    and so now I have to tell
That low in the ground, lying peaceful and still,
    is the other foot—
        And the rest of him as well.

*S. Taylor Harris*


### THE TWO OLD BACHELORS

Two old Bachelors were living in one house;
One caught a Muffin, the other caught a Mouse.
Said he who caught the Muffin to him who caught
    the Mouse,
"This happens just in time! For we've nothing in
    the house,
Save a tiny slice of lemon and a teaspoonful of
    honey.
And what to do for dinner—since we haven't any
    money?
And what can we expect if we haven't any dinner,
But to lose our teeth and eyelashes and keep on
    growing thinner?"
Said he who caught the Mouse to him who caught
    the Muffin,
"We might cook this little Mouse, if we only had
    some Stuffin'!
If we had but Sage and Onion we could do
    extremely well,
But how to get that Stuffin' it is difficult to
    tell!"

Those two old Bachelors ran quickly to the
town
And asked for Sage and Onion as they wandered
up and down;
They borrowed two large Onions, but no Sage
was to be found
In the Shops, or in the Market, or in all the
Gardens round.

But some one said, "A hill there is, a little to the
north,
And to its purpledicular top a narrow way leads
forth;
And there among the rugged rocks abides an
ancient Sage,
An earnest Man, who reads all day a most per-
plexing page.
Climb up, and seize him by the toes!—all studious
as he sits,
And pull him down—and chop him into endless
little bits!
Then mix him with your Onion (cut up likewise
into Scraps,)
When your Stuffin' will be ready—and very good:
perhaps."

Those two old Bachelors without loss of time
The nearly purpledicular crags at once began to
climb;
And at the top, among the rocks, all seated in a
nook,
They saw that Sage, a-reading of a most enormous
book.

H

"You earnest Sage!" aloud they cried, "your
   book you've read enough in!
We wish to chop you into bits to mix you into
   Stuffin'!"

But that old Sage looked calmly up, and with his
   awful book,
At those two Bachelors' bald heads a certain aim
   he took;
And over crag and precipice they rolled pro-
   miscuous down;
At once they rolled, and never stopped in lane or
   field or town;
And when they reached their house, they found
   (besides their want of Stuffin',)
The Mouse had fled; and, previously, had eaten
   up the Muffin.

They left their home in silence by the once
   convivial door.
And from that hour those Bachelors were never
   heard of more.

                                        *Edward Lear*


### MATILDA

*Who told Lies, and was Burned to Death*

MATILDA told such dreadful lies,
It made one gasp and stretch one's eyes;
Her aunt, who, from her earliest youth,
Had kept a strict regard for truth,

Attempted to believe Matilda:
The effort very nearly killed her,
And would have done so, had not she
Discovered this infirmity.
For once, towards the close of day,
    Matilda, growing tired of play,
And finding she was left alone,
Went tiptoe to the telephone,
And summoned the immediate aid
Of London's noble fire-brigade.
Within an hour the gallant band
Were pouring in on every hand
From Putney, Hackney Downs, and Bow
With courage high and hearts a-glow
They galloped, roaring through the town,
"Matilda's house is burning down!"
Inspired by British cheers and loud
Proceeding from the frenzied crowd,
They ran their ladders through a score
Of windows on the ballroom floor;
And took peculiar pains to souse
The pictures up and down the house,
Until Matilda's aunt succeeded
In showing them they were not needed.
And even then she had to pay
To get the men to go away!
    .        .        .        .        .

It happened that a few weeks later,
Her aunt was off to the theatre,
To see that interesting play,
*The Second Mrs Tanqueray*.
She had refused to take her niece
To hear this entertaining piece:

A deprivation just and wise,
To punish her for telling lies.
That night a fire *did* break out—
You should have heard Matilda shout!
You should have heard her scream and bawl,
And throw the window up, and call
To people passing in the street—
(The rapidly increasing heat
Encouraging her to obtain
Their confidence)—but all in vain!
For every time she shouted "Fire!"
They only answered "Little liar!"
And therefore, when her aunt returned,
Matilda, and the house, were burned.

*Hilaire Belloc*


### ELEGY ON THE DEATH OF A MAD DOG

GOOD people all, of every sort,
  Give ear unto my song;
And if you find it wondrous short,
  It cannot hold you long.

In Islington there was a man
  Of whom the world might say
That still a godly race he ran—
  Whene'er he went to pray.

A kind and gentle heart he had
  To comfort friends and foes;
The naked every day he clad—
  When he put on his clothes.

And in that town a dog was found
  As many dogs there be,
Both mongrel, puppy, whelp, and hound,
  And curs of low degree.

This dog and man at first were friends;
  But when a pique began,
The dog, to gain some private ends,
  Went mad, and bit the man.

Around from all the neighbouring streets
  The wondering neighbours ran,
And swore the dog had lost his wits
  To bite so good a man.

The wound it seemed both sore and sad
  To every Christian eye;
And while they swore the dog was mad,
  They swore the man would die.

But soon a wonder came to light,
  That showed the rogues they lied;
The man recovered of the bite—
  The dog it was that died.

*Oliver Goldsmith*

### ED. AND SID AND BERNARD

THE Hobson-Jobson children were enamoured of
  the sciences,
  A state of mind that may seem very queer;
They spent their pocket-money on the strangest
  of appliances
  And wasted none at all on ginger-beer.

Enterprising Edwin was expert in electricity,
　　Of batteries and lamps he had a stock;
He called his father "ampere" in his youthful
　　eccentricity,
　　Although his pa re-volted from the shock.

Systematic Sidney used to study the barometer
　　And all about fog, sunshine, snow, and rain;
He dabbled in hydraulics, too, and kept a pet
　　hydrometer,
　　And folks said he had water on the brain.

The other brother, Bernard, had a bias for biology,
　　He used to cut up worms and fish and frogs:
His shocked relations prophesied in vivid phrase-
　　ology
　　He'd go, when he was older, to the dogs.

But, though as children all of them enjoyed this
　　opportunity,
　　Young Bernard steaks and cutlets had to chop,
Sid became a plumber, stopping leaks for the
　　community,
　　And Edwin wrapped up currants in a shop.

*Edward MacDuff*


HIAWATHA'S PHOTOGRAPHING

From his shoulder Hiawatha
Took the camera of rosewood,
Made of sliding, folding rosewood;
Neatly put it all together.

In its case it lay compactly,
Folded into nearly nothing;
But he opened out the hinges,
Pushed and pulled the joints and hinges,
Till it looked all squares and oblongs,
Like a complicated figure
In the Second Book of Euclid.

This he perched upon a tripod—
Crouched beneath its dusky cover—
Stretched his hand, enforcing silence—
Said "Be motionless, I beg you!"
Mystic, awful was the process.

All the family in order
Sat before him for their pictures:
Each in turn, as he was taken,
Volunteered his own suggestions,
His ingenious suggestions.

First the Governor, the Father:
He suggested velvet curtains
Looped about a massy pillar;
And the corner of a table,
Of a rosewood dining-table.
He would hold a scroll of something,
Hold it firmly in his left-hand;
He would keep his right-hand buried
(Like Napoleon) in his waistcoat;
He would contemplate the distance
With a look of pensive meaning,
As of ducks that die in tempests.

Grand, heroic was the notion:
Yet the picture failed entirely:
Failed, because he moved a little;
Moved, because he couldn't help it.

Next, his better half took courage;
*She* would have her picture taken.
She came dressed beyond description,
Dressed in jewels and in satin
Far too gorgeous for an empress.
Gracefully she sat down sideways,
With a simper scarcely human,
Holding in her hand a bouquet
Rather larger than a cabbage.
All the while that she was sitting,
Still the lady chattered, chattered,
Like a monkey in the forest.
"Am I sitting still?" she asked him.
"Is my face enough in profile?
Shall I hold the bouquet higher?
Will it come into the picture?"
And the picture failed completely.

Next the son, the Stunning-Cantab:
He suggested curves of beauty,
Curves pervading all his figure,
Which the eye might follow onward,
Till they centred in the breast-pin,
Centred in the golden breast-pin.

He had learnt it all from Ruskin
(Author of *The Stones of Venice*,
*Seven Lamps of Architecture*,
*Modern Painters*, and some others);
And perhaps he had not fully
Understood his author's meaning;
But, whatever was the reason,
All was fruitless, as the picture
Ended in an utter failure.

Next to him the eldest daughter:

She suggested very little,
Only asked if he would take her
With her look of "passive beauty."
    Her idea of passive beauty
Was a squinting of the left eye,
Was a drooping of the right eye,
Was a smile that went up sideways
To the corner of the nostrils.
    Hiawatha, when she asked him,
Took no notice of the question,
Looked as if he hadn't heard it.
But, when pointedly appealed to,
Smiled in his peculiar manner,
Coughed, and said it "didn't matter,"
Bit his lip, and changed the subject.
    Nor in this was he mistaken,
As the picture failed completely.
    So in turn the other sisters.
    Last, the youngest son was taken:
Very rough and thick his hair was,
Very round and red his face was,
Very dusty was his jacket,
Very fidgety his manner.
And his overbearing sisters
Called him names he disapproved of:
Called him Johnny, "Daddy's darling,"
Called him Jacky, "Scrubby School-boy."
And, so awful was the picture,
In comparison the others
Seemed, to one's bewildered fancy,
To have partially succeeded.
    Finally my Hiawatha
Tumbled all the tribe together,

('Grouped' is not the right expression),
And, as happy chance would have it,
Did at last obtain a picture
Where the faces all succeeded:
Each came out a perfect likeness.
   Then they joined and all abused it,
Unrestrainedly abused it,
As the worst and ugliest picture
They could possibly have dreamed of.
"Giving one such strange expressions—
Sullen, stupid, pert expressions.
Really anyone would take us
(Anyone that did not know us)
For the most unpleasant people!"
(Hiawatha seemed to think so,
Seemed to think it not unlikely).
All together rang their voices,
Angry, loud, discordant voices,
As of dogs that howl in concert,
As of cats that wail in chorus.
   But my Hiawatha's patience,
His politeness and his patience,
Unaccountably had vanished,
And he left that happy party.
Neither did he leave them slowly,
With the calm deliberation,
The intense deliberation
Of a photographic artist:
But he left them in a hurry,
Left them in a mighty hurry,
Stating that he would not stand it,
Stating in emphatic language
What he'd be before he'd stand it.

Hurriedly he packed his boxes,
Hurriedly the porter trundled
On a barrow all his boxes:
Hurriedly he took his ticket:
Hurriedly the train received him:
Thus departed Hiawatha.

*Lewis Carroll*

# WONDER AND MAGIC

## THE THREE BEGGARS

'Twas autumn daybreak gold and wild;
　　While past St Ann's grey tower they shuffled
Three beggars spied a fairy-child
　　In crimson mantle muffled.

The daybreak lighted up her face
　　All pink, and sharp, and emerald-eyed;
She looked on them a little space,
　　And shrill as hautboy cried:

"O three tall footsore men of rags
　　Which walking this gold morn I see,
What will ye give me from your bags
　　For fairy kisses three?"

The first, that was a reddish man,
　　Out of his bundle takes a crust:
"La, by the tombstones of St Ann,
　　There's fee, if fee ye must!"

The second, that was a chestnut man,
　　Out of his bundle draws a bone:
"La, by the belfry of St Ann,
　　And all my breakfast gone!"

The third, that was a yellow man,
　　Out of his bundle picks a groat:
"La, by the Angel of St Ann,
　　And I must go without."

That changeling, lean and icy-lipped,
  Touched crust, and bone, and groat, and lo!
Beneath her finger, taper-tipped,
  The magic all ran through.

Instead of crust, a peacock pie,
  Instead of bone, sweet venison,
Instead of groat, a white lily
  With seven blooms thereon.

And each fair cup was deep with wine:
  Such was the changeling's charity,
The sweet feast was enough for nine,
  But not too much for three.

O toothsome meat in jelly froze!
  O tender haunch of elfin stag!
O rich the odour that arose!
  O plump with scraps each bag!

There, in the daybreak gold and wild,
  Each merry-hearted beggar-man
Drank deep unto the fairy child,
  And blessed the good St Ann.

*Walter de la Mare*

### THE NECKAN

In summer on the headlands,
  The Baltic Sea along,
Sits Neckan with his harp of gold,
  And sings his plaintive song.

Green rolls beneath the headlands,
    Green rolls the Baltic Sea;
And there below the Neckan's feet,
    His wife and children be.

He sings not of the ocean,
    Its shells and roses pale;
Of earth, of earth the Neckan sings,
    He hath no other tale.

He sits upon the headlands,
    And sings a mournful stave
Of all he saw and felt on earth
    Far from the kind sea-wave.

Sings how, a knight, he wandered
    By castle, field and town—
But earthly knights have harder hearts
    Than the sea-children own.

Sings of his earthly bridal—
    Priest, knights, and ladies gay.
"And who art thou," the priest began,
    "Sir Knight, who wedd'st to-day?"—

"I am no knight," he answered;
    "From the sea-waves I come."—
The knights drew sword, the ladies screamed,
    The surpliced priest stood dumb.

He sings how from the chapel
    He vanished with his bride,
And bore her down to the sea-halls,
    Beneath the salt sea-tide.

He sings how she sits weeping
   'Mid shells that round her lie.
"False Neckan shares my bed," she weeps,
   "No Christian mate have I."—

He sings how through the billows
   He rose to earth again,
And sought a priest to sign the cross,
   That Neckan Heaven might gain.

He sings how, on an evening,
   Beneath the birch-trees cool,
He sat and played his harp of gold,
   Beside the river-pool.

Beside the pool sat Neckan,
   Tears filled his mild blue eye;
On his white mule, across the bridge,
   A cassocked priest rode by.

"Why sitt'st thou there, O Neckan,
   And play'st thy harp of gold?
Sooner shall this my staff bear leaves,
   Than thou shalt Heaven behold."

But, lo, the staff it budded!
   It greened, it branched, it waved.
"O ruth of God," the priest cried out,
   "This lost sea-creature saved!"

The cassocked priest rode onwards,
   And vanished with his mule;
But Neckan in the twilight grey
   Wept by the river-pool.

He wept: "The earth hath kindness,
  The sea, the starry poles;
Earth, sea and sky, and God above—
  But, ah, not human souls!"

In summer, on the headlands,
  The Baltic Sea along,
Sits Neckan with his harp of gold,
  And sings this plaintive song.

*Matthew Arnold*


### ALICE BRAND

#### I

MERRY it is in the good greenwood,
  When the mavis and merle are singing,
When the deer sweeps by, and the hounds are
    in cry,
  And the hunter's horn is ringing.

"O Alice Brand, my native land
  Is lost for love of you;
And we must hold by wood and wold,
  As outlaws wont to do.

"O Alice, 'twas all for thy locks so bright,
  And 'twas all for thine eyes so blue,
That on the night of our luckless flight
  Thy brother bold I slew.

"Now must I teach to hew the beech
    The hand that held the glaive,
For leaves to spread our lowly bed,
    And stakes to fence our cave.

"And for vest of pall, thy fingers small
    That wont on harp to stray,
A cloak must shear from the slaughtered deer,
    To keep the cold away."

"O Richard! if my brother died,
    'Twas but a fatal chance,
For darkling was the battle tried,
    And fortune sped the lance.

"If pall and vair[1] no more I wear,
    Nor thou the crimson sheen,
As warm, we'll say, is the russet grey,
    As gay the forest green.

"And Richard, if our lot be hard,
    And lost thy native land,
Still Alice has her own Richard,
    And he his Alice Brand."

II

'Tis merry, 'tis merry, in good greenwood,
    So blithe Lady Alice is singing;
On the beech's pride, and oak's brown side,
    Lord Richard's axe is ringing.

[1] *Vair*, a kind of fur.

Up spoke the moody Elfin King,
  Who woned within the hill—
Like wind in the porch of a ruined church,
  His voice was ghostly shrill.

"Why sounds yon stroke on beech and oak,
  Our moonlight circle's screen?
Or who comes here to chase the deer,
  Beloved of our Elfin Queen?
Or who may dare on wold to wear
  The fairies' fatal green?

"Up, Urgan, up! to yon mortal hie,
  For thou wert christened man;
For cross or sign thou wilt not fly,
  For muttered word or ban.

"Lay on him the curse of the withered heart,
  The curse of the sleepless eye;
Till he wish and pray that his life would part,
  Nor yet find leave to die!"

### III

'Tis merry, 'tis merry, in good greenwood,
  Though the birds have stilled their singing;
The evening blaze doth Alice raise,
  And Richard is fagots bringing.

Up Urgan starts, that hideous dwarf,
  Before Lord Richard stands,
And, as he crossed, and blessed himself,
  "I fear not sign," quoth the grisly elf,
  "That is made with bloody hands."

But out then spoke she, Alice Brand,
  That woman void of fear—
"And if there's blood upon his hand,
  'Tis but the blood of deer."

"Now loud thou liest, thou bold of mood!
  It cleaves unto his hand,
The stain of thine own kindly blood,
  The blood of Ethert Brand."

Then forward stepped she, Alice Brand,
  And made the holy sign;
"And if there's blood on Richard's hand,
  A spotless hand is mine.

"And I conjure thee, Demon elf,
  By Him whom Demons fear,
To show us whence thou art thyself,
  And what thine errand here?"

### IV

" 'Tis merry, 'tis merry, in Fairyland,
  When fairy birds are singing,
When the court doth ride by the monarch's
    side,
  With bit and bridle ringing:

"And gaily shines the Fairyland—
  But all is glistening show,
Like the idle gleam that December's beam
  Can dart on ice and snow.

"And fading, like that varied gleam,
　　Is our inconstant shape,
Who now like knight and lady seem,
　　And now like dwarf and ape.

"It was between the night and day,
　　When the Fairy King has power,
That I sunk down in a sinful fray,
And, 'twixt life and death, was snatched
　　　away
　　To the joyless Elfin bower.

"But wist I of a woman bold,
　　Who thrice my brow durst sign,
I might regain my mortal mould,
　　As fair a form as thine."

She crossed him once—she crossed him twice—
　　The lady was so brave;
The fouler grew his goblin hue,
　　The darker grew the cave.

She crossed him thrice, that lady bold;
　　He rose beneath her hand
The fairest knight on Scottish mould,
　　Her brother, Ethert Brand!

Merry it is in good greenwood,
　　When the mavis and merle are singing,
But merrier were they in Dunfermline grey,
　　When all the bells were ringing.

*Sir Walter Scott*

## THE BALLAD OF SEMMERWATER

### [*A North-Country Legend*]

DEEP asleep, deep asleep,
  Deep asleep it lies,
The still lake of Semmerwater
  Under the still skies.

And many a fathom, many a fathom,
  Many a fathom below,
In a king's tower and a queen's bower
  The fishes come and go.

Once there stood by Semmerwater
  A mickle town and tall;
King's tower and queen's bower,
  And the wakeman on the wall.

Came a beggar halt and sore:
  "I faint for lack of bread."
King's tower and queen's bower
  Cast him forth unfed.

He knocked at the door of the herdman's cot,
  The herdman's cot in the dale,
They gave him of their oatcake,
  They gave him of their ale.

He has cursed aloud that city proud,
  He has cursed it in its pride;
He has cursed it into Semmerwater
  Down the brant hillside;
He has cursed it into Semmerwater,
  There to bide.

King's tower and queen's bower,
   And a mickle town and tall;
By glimmer of scale and gleam of fin,
   Folk have seen them all.

King's tower and queen's bower,
   And weed and reed in the gloom;
And a lost city in Semmerwater,
   Deep asleep till Doom.

*Sir William Watson*


### KALLUNDBORG CHURCH

"BUILD at Kallundborg by the sea
A church as stately as church may be,
And there shalt thou wed my daughter fair,"
Said the Lord of Nesvek to Esbern Snare.

And the Baron laughed. But Esbern said,
"Though I lose my soul, I will Helva wed!"
And off he strode, in his pride of will,
To the Troll who dwelt in Ulshoi hill.

"Build, O Troll, a church for me
At Kallundborg by the mighty sea;
Build it stately, and build it fair,
Build it quickly," said Esbern Snare.

But the sly Dwarf said, "No work is wrought
By Trolls of the Hills, O man, for nought.
What wilt thou give for thy church so fair?"
"Set thine own price," quoth Esbern Snare.

"When Kallundborg church is builded well,
Thou must the name of its builder tell,
Or thy heart and thy eyes must be my boon."
"Build," said Esbern, "and build it soon."

By night and by day the Troll wrought on;
He hewed the timbers, he piled the stone;
But day by day, as the walls rose fair,
Darker and sadder grew Esbern Snare.

Of his evil bargain far and wide
A rumour ran through the countryside;
And Helva of Nesvek, young and fair,
Prayed for the soul of Esbern Snare.

And now the church was well-nigh done;
One pillar it lacked, and one alone;
And the grim Troll muttered, "Fool thou art!
To-morrow gives me thy eyes and heart!"

By Kallundborg in black despair,
Through wood and meadow walked Esbern Snare,
Till, worn and weary, the strong man sank
Under the birches on Ulshoi bank.

At his last day's work he heard the Troll
Hammer and delve in the quarry's hole;
Before him the church stood large and fair;
"I have builded my tomb," said Esbern Snare.

And he closed his eyes the sight to hide,
When he heard a light step at his side:
"O Esbern Snare!" a sweet voice said,
"Would I might die now in thy stead!"

With a grasp by love and by fear made strong,
He held her fast, and he held her long;
With the beating heart of a bird afeard,
She hid her face in his flame-red beard.

"O Love!" he cried, "let me look to-day
In thine eyes, ere mine are plucked away;
Let me hold thee close, let me feel thy heart,
Ere mine by the Troll is torn apart!

"I sinned, O Helva, for love of thee!
Pray that the Lord Christ pardon me!"
But fast as she prayed, and faster still,
Hammered the Troll in Ulshoi hill.

He knew, as he wrought, that a loving heart
Was somehow baffling his evil art;
For more than spell of Elf or Troll
Is a maiden's prayer for her lover's soul.

And Esbern listened, and caught the sound
Of a Troll-wife singing underground:
"To-morrow comes Fine, father thine;
Lie still and hush thee, baby mine!

"Lie still, my darling! next sunrise
Thou'lt play with Esbern Snare's heart and eyes!"
"Ho! ho!" quoth Esbern, "is that your game?
Thanks to the Troll-wife, I know his name!"

The Troll he heard him, and hurried on
To Kallundborg church with the lacking stone.
"Too late, Gaffer Fine!" cried Esbern Snare;
And Troll and pillar vanished in air!

That night the harvesters heard the sound
Of a woman sobbing underground,
And the voice of the Hill-Troll loud with blame
Of the careless singer who told his name.

Of the Troll of the church they sing the rune
By the Northern Sea in the harvest moon;
And the fishers of Zealand hear him still
Scolding his wife in Ulshoi hill.

And seaward over its groves of birch
Still looks the tower of Kallundborg church,
Where, first at its altar, a wedded pair,
Stood Helva of Nesvek and Esbern Snare!

*John Greenleaf Whittier*

### THE PIED PIPER OF HAMELIN

HAMELIN Town's in Brunswick,
  By famous Hanover city;
The river Weser, deep and wide,
Washes its wall on the southern side;
A pleasanter spot you never spied;
  But, when begins my ditty,
Almost five hundred years ago,
To see the townsfolk suffer so
  From vermin was a pity.

  Rats!
They fought the dogs, and killed the cats,
  And bit the babies in the cradles,
And ate the cheeses out of the vats,
  And licked the soup from the cooks' own ladles,

Split open the kegs of salted sprats,
Made nests inside men's Sunday hats,
And even spoiled the women's chats
    By drowning their speaking
    With shrieking and squeaking
In fifty different sharps and flats.

At last the people in a body
    To the Town Hall came flocking:
" 'Tis clear," cried they, "our Mayor's a
        noddy;
    And as for our Corporation—shocking
To think we buy gowns lined with ermine
For dolts that can't or won't determine
What's best to rid us of our vermin!
You hope, because you're old and obese,
To find in the furry civic robe ease?
Rouse up, sirs! Give your brains a racking
To find the remedy we're lacking,
Or, sure as fate, we'll send you packing!"
At this the Mayor and Corporation
Quaked with a mighty consternation.

An hour they sate in council;
    At length the Mayor broke silence:
"For a guilder I'd my ermine gown sell;
    I wish I were a mile hence!
It's easy to bid one rack one's brain—
I'm sure my poor head aches again
I've scratched it so, and all in vain.
Oh for a trap, a trap, a trap!"
Just as he said this, what should hap
At the chamber door but a gentle tap?

"Bless us," cried the Mayor, "what's that?
Only a scraping of shoes on the mat?
Anything like the sound of a rat
Makes my heart go pit-a-pat!"

"Come in!" the Mayor cried, looking bigger;
And in did come the strangest figure!
His queer long coat from heel to head
Was half of yellow and half of red;
And he himself was tall and thin,
With sharp blue eyes, each like a pin,
And light loose hair, yet swarthy skin,
No tuft on cheek nor beard on chin,
But lips where smiles went out and in—
There was no guessing his kith and kin!
And nobody could enough admire
The tall man and his quaint attire.
Quoth one: "It's as my great-grandsire,
Starting up at the Trump of Doom's tone,
Had walked this way from his painted tomb-
        stone!"

He advanced to the council-table:
And, "Please your honours," said he, "I'm
        able,
By means of a secret charm, to draw
    All creatures living beneath the sun
    That creep, or swim, or fly, or run,
After me so as you never saw!
And I chiefly use my charm
On creatures that do people harm,
The mole, and toad, and newt, and viper,
And people call me the Pied Piper."

(And here they noticed round his neck
   A scarf of red and yellow stripe,
To match with his coat of the self-same check;
   And at the scarf's end hung a pipe;
And his fingers, they noticed, were ever stray-
     ing
As if impatient to be playing
Upon this pipe, as low it dangled
Over his vesture so old-fangled.)
"Yet," said he, "poor piper as I am,
In Tartary I freed the Cham,
   Last June, from his huge swarms of gnats;
I eased in Asia the Nizam
   Of a monstrous brood of vampire-bats;
And, as for what your brain bewilders—
   If I can rid your town of rats
Will you give me a thousand guilders?"
"One? fifty thousand!" was the exclamation
Of the astonished Mayor and Corporation.

Into the street the Piper stepped,
   Smiling first a little smile,
As if he knew what magic slept
   In his quiet pipe the while;
Then, like a musical adept,
To blow the pipe his lips he wrinkled,
And green and blue his sharp eyes twinkled,
Like a candle-flame when salt is sprinkled;
And ere three shrill notes the pipe uttered,
You heard as if an army muttered;
And the muttering grew to a grumbling;
And the grumbling grew to a mighty rumbling;
And out of the houses the rats came tumbling.

Great rats, small rats, lean rats, brawny rats,
Brown rats, black rats, grey rats, tawny rats,
Grave old plodders, gay young friskers,
    Fathers, mothers, uncles, cousins,
Cocking tails and pricking whiskers,
    Families by tens and dozens,
Brothers, sisters, husbands, wives—
Followed the Piper for their lives.
From street to street he piped advancing,
And step by step they followed dancing,
Until they came to the river Weser,
    Wherein all plunged and perished!
—Save one, who, stout as Julius Caesar,
Swam across and lived to carry
    (As he the manuscript he cherished)
To Rat-land home his commentary,
Which was, "At the first shrill notes of the
      pipe,
I heard a sound as of scraping tripe,
And putting apples, wondrous ripe,
Into a cider-press's gripe,
And a moving away of pickle-tub boards,
And a leaving ajar of conserve cupboards,
And a drawing the corks of train-oil flasks,
And a breaking the hoops of butter-casks;
And it seemed as if a voice
    (Sweeter far than by harp or by psaltery
Is breathed) called out, 'O, rats, rejoice!
    The world is grown to one vast drysaltery!
So munch on, crunch on, take your nuncheon,
Breakfast, supper, dinner, luncheon!'
And just as a bulky sugar-puncheon,
All ready stewed, like a great sun shone

Glorious, scarce an inch before me,
Just as methought it said, 'Come, bore me!'
—I found the Weser rolling o'er me."

You should have heard the Hamelin people
Ringing the bells till they rocked the steeple;
"Go," cried the Mayor, "and get long poles!
Poke out the nests and block up the holes!
Consult with carpenters and builders,
And leave in our town not even a trace
Of the rats!"—when suddenly, up the face
Of the piper perked in the market place,
With a, "First, if you please, my thousand
    guilders!"

A thousand guilders! The Mayor looked blue;
So did the Corporation too.
For council dinners made rare havoc
With Claret, Moselle, Vin-de-Grave, Hock;
And half the money would replenish
Their cellar's biggest butt with Rhenish.
To pay this sum to a wandering fellow
With a gipsy coat of red and yellow!
"Besides," quoth the Mayor with a knowing wink,
"Our business was done at the river's brink;
We saw with our eyes the vermin sink,
And what's dead can't come to life, I think.
So, friend, we're not the folks to shrink
From the duty of giving you something to drink,
And a matter of money to put in your poke;
But, as for the guilders, what we spoke
Of them, as you very well know, was in joke.
Beside, our losses have made us thrifty;
A thousand guilders! Come, take fifty!"

The Piper's face fell, and he cried,
"No trifling! I can't wait! beside,
I've promised to visit by dinner-time
Bagdat, and accept the prime
Of the Head Cook's potage, all he's rich in,
For having left, in the Caliph's kitchen,
Of a nest of scorpions no survivor—
With him I proved no bargain-driver;
With you, don't think I'll bate a stiver!
And folks who put me in a passion
May find me pipe after another fashion."

"How?" cried the Mayor, "d'ye think I brook
Being worse treated than a Cook?
Insulted by a lazy ribald
With idle pipe and vesture piebald?
You threaten us, fellow? Do your worst:
Blow your pipe there till you burst!"

Once more he stepped into the street,
    And to his lips again
    Laid his long pipe of smooth straight cane;
And ere he blew three notes (such sweet
Soft notes as yet musicians cunning
    Never gave the enraptured air)
There was a rustling, that seemed like a bustling
Of many crowds justling, at pitching and hustling;
Small feet were pattering, wooden shoes clatter-
        ing,
Little hands clapping, and little tongues chatter-
        ing;
And like fowls in a farmyard when barley is
        scattering,

Out came the children running:
All the little boys and girls,
With rosy cheeks and flaxen curls,
And sparkling eyes and teeth like pearls,
Tripping and skipping, ran merrily after
The wonderful music with shouting and
    laughter.

The Mayor was dumb, and the Council stood
As if they were changed into blocks of wood,
Unable to move a step, or cry
To the children merrily skipping by,
—Could only follow with the eye
That joyous crowd at the Piper's back.
But how the Mayor was on the rack,
And the wretched Council's bosoms beat,
As the Piper turned from the High Street
To where the Weser rolled its waters
Right in the way of their sons and daughters!
However, he turned from south to west,
And to Koppelberg Hill his steps addressed,
And after him the children pressed.
Great was the joy in every breast:
"He never can cross that mighty top!
He's forced to let the piping drop,
And we shall see our children stop!"
When, lo, as they reached the mountain-side,
A wondrous portal opened wide,
As if a cavern was suddenly hollowed;
And the Piper advanced and the children
    followed;
And when all were in, to the very last,
The door in the mountain-side shut fast.

Did I say, all?  No! one was lame,
    And could not dance the whole of the way;
And in after years, if you would blame
    His sadness, he was used to say—
"It's dull in our town since my playmates
    left!
I can't forget that I'm bereft
Of all the pleasant sights they see,
Which the Piper also promised me;
For he led us, he said, to a joyous land,
Joining the town and just at hand,
Where waters gushed and fruit-trees grew,
And flowers put forth a fairer hue,
And everything was strange and new;
The sparrows were brighter than peacocks here,
And their dogs outran our fallow deer,
And honey-bees had lost their stings,
And horses were born with eagles' wings;
And just as I became assured
My lame foot would be speedily cured,
The music stopped, and I stood still
And found myself outside the hill,
Left alone against my will,
To go now limping as before
And never hear of that country more!"

Alas, alas for Hamelin!
    There came into many a burgher's pate
    A text which says that heaven's gate
    Opes to the rich at as easy rate,
As the needle's eye takes a camel in!
The Mayor sent East, West, North, and South,
To offer the Piper by word of mouth,

K

Wherever it was men's lot to find him,
Silver and gold to his heart's content,
If he'd only return the way he went,
   And bring the children behind him.
But when they saw 'twas a lost endeavour,
And piper and dancers were gone for ever,
They made a decree that lawyers never
   Should think their records dated duly
If, after the date of the month and year,
These words did not as well appear,
   "And so long after what happened here
   On the twenty-second of July,
   Thirteen hundred and seventy-six."
And the better in memory to fix
The place of the children's last retreat,
They called it, the Pied Piper's Street—
Where any one playing on pipe or tabor,
Was sure for the future to lose his labour.
Nor suffered they hostelry or tavern
   To shock with mirth a street so solemn;
But opposite the place of the cavern
   They wrote the story on a column,
And on the great church-window painted
The same, to make the world acquainted
How their children were stolen away;
And there it stands to this very day.
And I must not omit to say
That in Transylvania there's a tribe
Of alien people who ascribe
The outlandish ways and dress
On which their neighbours lay such stress,
To their fathers' and mothers' having risen
Out of some subterraneous prison

Into which they were trepanned
Long ago in a mighty band
Out of Hamelin town in Brunswick land;
But how or why, they don't understand.

So, Willy, let you and me be wipers
Of scores out with all men—especially pipers!
And whether they pipe us free from rats or
    from mice,
If we've promised them aught, let us keep our
    promise!

*Robert Browning*

# ECHOES OF HISTORY

## THE DANES

THEIR sails, as black as a starless night,
Came moving on, with a sullen might;
Rows of gleaming shields there hung,
Over the gunwales in order slung;
And the broad black banners fluttered and flapped
Like raven's pinions, as dipped and lapped
The Norsemen's galleys; their axes shone;

Every Dane had a hauberk on—
Glittering gold; how each robber lord
Waved in the air his threatening sword!
One long swift rush through surf and foam
And they leapt, ere the rolling wave had gone,
On our Saxon shore, their new-found home.

*G. W. Thornbury*

## THE ARMADA

ATTEND, all ye who list to hear our noble England's
    praise;
I tell of the thrice famous deeds she wrought in
    ancient days,
When that great fleet invincible against her bore
    in vain
The richest spoils of Mexico, the stoutest hearts of
    Spain.

It was about the lovely close of a warm summer
day,
There came a gallant merchant-ship full sail to
Plymouth Bay;
Her crew hath seen Castile's black fleet, beyond
Aurigny's isle,
At earliest twilight, on the waves lie heaving many
a mile.·
At sunrise she escaped their van, by God's especial
grace;
And the tall *Pinta*, till the noon, had held her
close in chase.
Forthwith a guard at every gun was placed along
the wall;
The beacon blazed upon the roof of Edgecumbe's
lofty hall;
Many a light fishing-bark put out to pry along the
coast,
And with loose rein and bloody spur rode inland
many a post.
With his white hair unbonneted, the stout old
sheriff comes;
Behind him march the halberdiers; before him
sound the drums;
His yeomen round the market cross make clear an
ample space;
For there behoves him to set up the standard of
Her Grace.
And haughtily the trumpets peal, and gaily dance
the bells,
As slow upon the labouring wind the royal blazon
swells.

Look how the Lion of the sea lifts up his ancient
    crown,
And underneath his deadly paw treads the gay
    lilies down!
So stalked he when he turned to flight, on that
    famed Picard field,
Bohemia's plume, and Genoa's bow, and Caesar's
    eagle shield.
So glared he when at Agincourt in wrath he
    turned to bay,
And crushed and torn beneath his claws the
    princely hunters lay.
Ho! strike the flagstaff deep, Sir Knight: ho!
    scatter flowers, fair maids:
Ho! gunners, fire a loud salute: ho! gallants, draw
    your blades:
Thou sun, shine on her joyously: ye breezes, waft
    her wide;
Our glorious SEMPER EADEM, the banner of our
    pride.

The freshening breeze of eve unfurled that
    banner's massy fold;
The parting gleam of sunshine kissed that haughty
    scroll of gold;
Night sank upon the dusky beach, and on the
    purple sea,
Such night in England ne'er had been, nor e'er
    again shall be.
From Eddystone to Berwick bounds, from Lynn
    to Milford Bay,
That time of slumber was as bright and busy as
    the day;

For swift to east and swift to west the ghastly
war-flame spread,
High on St Michael's Mount it shone: it shone on
Beachy Head.
Far on the deep the Spaniard saw, along each
southern shire,
Cape beyond cape, in endless range, those twink-
ling points of fire.
The fisher left his skiff to rock on Tamar's glitter-
ing waves;
The rugged miners poured to war from Mendip's
sunless caves;
O'er Longleat's towers, o'er Cranbourne's oaks,
the fiery herald flew;
He roused the shepherds of Stonehenge, the
rangers of Beaulieu.
Right sharp and quick the bells all night rang out
from Bristol town,
And ere the day three hundred horse had met on
Clifton Down;
The sentinel on Whitehall gate looked forth into
the night,
And saw, o'erhanging Richmond Hill, the streak
of blood-red light;
Then bugle's note and cannon's roar the death-
like silence broke,
And with one start, and with one cry, the royal
city woke.
At once on all her stately gates arose the answering
fires;
At once the wild alarum clashed from all her
reeling spires;

From all the batteries of the Tower pealed loud
    the voice of fear;
And all the thousand masts of Thames sent back
    a louder cheer;
And from the furthest wards was heard the rush of
    hurrying feet,
And the broad streams of pikes and flags rushed
    down each roaring street;
And broader still became the blaze, and louder
    still the din,
As fast from every village round the horse came
    spurring in.
And eastward straight from wild Blackheath the
    warlike errand went,
And roused in many an ancient hall the gallant
    squires of Kent.
Southward from Surrey's pleasant hills flew those
    bright couriers forth;
High on bleak Hampstead's swarthy moor they
    started for the north;
And on, and on, without a pause, untired they
    bounded still;
All night from tower to tower they sprang; they
    sprang from hill to hill;
Till the proud Peak unfurled the flag o'er Darwin's
    rocky dales,
Till like volcanoes flared to heaven the stormy hills
    of Wales,
Till twelve fair counties saw the blaze on Malvern's
    lonely height,
Till streamed in crimson on the wind the Wrekin's
    crest of light,

Till broad and fierce the star came forth on Ely's
    stately fane,
And tower and hamlet rose in arms o'er all the
    boundless plain;
Till Belvoir's lordly terraces the sign to Lincoln
    sent,
And Lincoln sped the message on o'er the wide
    vale of Trent;
Till Skiddaw saw the fire that burned on Gaunt's
    embattled pile,
And the red glare on Skiddaw roused the burghers
    of Carlisle.

*Lord Macaulay*

### AFTER BLENHEIM

IT was a summer evening;
    Old Kaspar's work was done,
And he before his cottage-door
    Was sitting in the sun;
And by him sported on the green
    His little grandchild, Wilhelmine.

She saw her brother Peterkin
    Roll something large and round,
Which he beside the rivulet
    In playing there, had found;
He came to ask what he had found,
That was so large, and smooth, and
    round.

Old Kaspar took it from the boy,
　Who stood expectant by;
And then the old man shook his head,
　And with a natural sigh—
" 'Tis some poor fellow's skull," said he,
"Who fell in the great victory.

"I find them in my garden,
　For there's many here about;
And often when I go to plough
　The ploughshare turns them out;
For many a thousand men," said he,
"Were slain in that great victory."

"Now tell us what 'twas all about,"
　Young Peterkin, he cries;
And little Wilhelmine looks up
　With wonder-waiting eyes;
"Now tell us all about the war,
And what they fought each other for."

"It was the English," Kaspar cried,
　"Who put the French to rout;
But what they fought each other for
　I could not well make out.
But everybody said," quoth he,
"That 'twas a famous victory.

"My father lived at Blenheim then,
　Yon little stream hard by;
They burnt his dwelling to the ground,
　And he was forced to fly;

So with his wife and child he fled,
Nor had he where to rest his head.


"With fire and sword the country round
    Was wasted far and wide,
And many a childing mother then,
    And new-born baby, died:
But things like that, you know, must be
At every famous victory.


"They say it was a shocking sight
    After the field was won;
For many thousand bodies here
    Lay rotting in the sun;
But things like that, you know, must be
After a famous victory.


"Great praise the Duke of Marlbro' won,
    And our good Prince Eugene."
"Why, 'twas a very wicked thing!"
    Said little Wilhelmine.
"Nay, nay, my little girl," quoth he,
"It was a famous victory.


"And everybody praised the Duke
    Who this great fight did win."
"But what good came of it at last?"
    Quoth little Peterkin.
"Why that I cannot tell," said he,
"But 'twas a famous victory."

*Robert Southey*

MOY CASTLE

*A Story of the '45*

THERE are seven men in Moy Castle
    Are merry men this night;
There are seven men in Moy Castle
    Whose hearts are gay and light.

Prince Charlie came to Moy Castle,
    And asked for shelter there,
And down came Lady M'Intosh,
    As proud as she was fair.

"I'm a hunted man, Lady M'Intosh—
    A price is on my head!
If Lord Loudon knew thou'dst sheltered me,
    Both thou and I were sped."

"Come in! come in, my prince!" said she,
    And opened wide the gate;
"To die with Prince Charlie Stuart,
    I ask no better fate."

She's called her seven trusty men,
    The blacksmith at their head:
"Ye shall keep watch in the castle wood,
    To save your prince from dread."

The lady has led the prince away,
    To make him royal cheer;
The seven men of M'Intosh
    Have sought the forest drear.

And there they looked and listened,
  Listened and looked amain;
And they heard the falling of the leaves,
  And the soft sound of the rain.

The blacksmith knelt beside an oak,
  And laid his ear to the ground,
And under the noises of the wood
  He heard a distant sound.

He heard the sound of many feet
  Warily treading the heather;
He heard a sound of many men
  Marching softly together.

"There's no time now to warn the prince,
  The castle guards are few;
'Tis wit will win the play to-night,
  And what we here can do."

He's gien the word to his six brethren,
  And through the wood they're gone;
The seven men of M'Intosh
  Each stood by himself alone.

"And he who has the pipes at his back,
  His best now let him play;
And he who has no pipes at his back,
  His best word let him say."

It was five hundred Englishmen
  Were treading the purple heather,
Five hundred of Lord Loudon's men
  Marching softly together.

"There's none to-night in Moy Castle
    But servants poor and old;
If we bring the prince to Loudon's lord,
    He'll fill our hands with gold."

They came lightly on their way,
    Had never a thought of ill,
When suddenly from the darksome wood
    Broke out a whistle shrill.

And straight the wood was filled with cries,
    With shouts of angry men,
And the angry skirl of the bagpipes
    Came answering the shouts again.

The Englishmen looked and listened,
    Listened and looked amain,
And nought could they see through the mirk
      night,
    But the pipes shrieked out again.

"Hark to the slogan of Lochiel,
    To Keppoch's gathering cry!
Hark to the rising swell that tells
    Clanranald's men are nigh!

"Now woe to the men that told us
    Lochiel was far away!
The whole of the Highland army
    Is waiting to bar our way.

"It's little we'll see of Charlie Stuart,
    And little of Loudon's gold,
And but we're away from this armèd wood,
    Our lives have but little hold."

It was five hundred Englishmen,
   They turned their faces and ran,
And well for him with the swiftest foot,
   For he was the lucky man.

And woe to him who was lame or slow
   For they trampled him on the heather!
And back to the place from whence they
      came
   They're hirpling all together.

Lord Loudon's men, they are gone full far
   Over the brow of the hill;
The seven men of M'Intosh,
   Their pipes are crying still.

They leaned them to a tree and laughed,
   'Twould do ye good to hear,
And they are away to Moy Castle,
   To tell their lady dear.

And who but Lady M'Intosh
   Would praise her men so bold?
And who but Prince Charlie Stuart
   Would count the good French gold?

There are seven men in Moy Castle
   Are joyful men this night;
There are seven men in Moy Castle
   Whose hearts will aye be light.

*Anonymous*

### THE BURIAL OF SIR JOHN MOORE

Not a drum was heard, not a funeral note,
   As his corse to the ramparts we hurried;
Not a soldier discharged his farewell shot,
   O'er the grave where our hero we buried.

We buried him darkly at dead of night,
   The sods with our bayonets turning,
By the struggling moonbeam's misty light,
   And the lantern dimly burning.

No useless coffin enclosed his breast,
   Nor in sheet nor in shroud we wound him,
But he lay like a warrior taking his rest,
   With his martial cloak around him.

Few and short were the prayers we said,
   And we spoke not a word of sorrow;
But we steadfastly gazed on the face of the dead,
   And we bitterly thought of the morrow.

We thought, as we hollowed his narrow bed,
   And smoothed down his lonely pillow,
That the foe and the stranger would tread o'er
     his head,
   And we far away on the billow!

Lightly they'll talk of the spirit that's gone,
   And o'er his cold ashes upbraid him;
But little he'll reck, if they let him sleep on
   In the grave where a Briton has laid him.

But half of our heavy task was done
  When the clock struck the hour for retiring;
And we heard the distant and random gun
  That the foe was sullenly firing.

Slowly and sadly we laid him down,
  From the field of his fame fresh and gory;
We carved not a line, and we raised not a stone,
  But we left him alone with his glory.

*Charles Wolfe*


## THE PIPES AT LUCKNOW

Pipes of the misty moorlands,
  Voice of the glens and hills;
The droning of the torrents,
  The treble of the rills!
Not the braes of broom and heather,
  Nor the mountains dark with rain,
Nor maiden bower, nor border tower,
  Have heard your sweetest strain!

Dear to the Lowland reaper,
  And plaided mountaineer,—
To the cottage and the castle
  The Scottish pipes are dear;
Sweet sounds the ancient pibroch
  O'er mountain, loch, and glade;
But the sweetest of all music
  The pipes at Lucknow played.

L

Day and night the Indian tiger
    Louder yelled, and nearer crept;
Round and round the jungle-serpent
    Near and nearer circles swept.
"Pray for rescue, wives and mothers—
    Pray to-day!" the soldier said;
"To-morrow, death's between us
    And the wrong and shame we dread."


Oh, they listened, looked, and waited,
    Till their hope became despair;
And the sobs of low bewailing
    Filled the pauses of their prayer.
Then up spake a Scottish maiden,
    With her ear unto the ground:
"Dinna ye hear it?—dinna ye hear it?
    The pipes o' Havelock sound!"


Hushed the wounded man his groaning;
    Hushed the wife her little ones;
Alone they heard the drum-roll
    And the roar of Sepoy guns.
But to sounds of home and childhood
    The Highland ear was true;
As her mother's cradle-crooning
    The mountain pipes she knew.


Like the march of soundless music
    Through the vision of the seer,
More of feeling than of hearing,
    Of the heart than of the ear,

She knew the droning pibroch,
   She knew the Campbell's call:
"Hark! hear ye no' MacGregor's,
   The grandest o' them all!"


Oh, they listened, dumb and breathless,
   And they caught the sound at last;
Faint and far beyond the Goomtee
   Rose and fell the piper's blast!
Then a burst of wild thanksgiving
   Mingled woman's voice and man's;
"God be praised!—the march of Havelock!
   The piping of the clans!"


Louder, nearer, fierce as vengeance,
   Sharp and shrill as swords at strife,
Came the wild MacGregor's clan-call,
   Stinging all the air to life.
But when the far-off dust-cloud
   To plaided legions grew,
Full tenderly and blithesomely
   The pipes of rescue blew!


Round the silver domes of Lucknow,
   Moslem mosque and Pagan shrine,
Breathed the air to Britons dearest,
   The air of Auld Lang Syne.
O'er the cruel roll of war-drums
   Rose that sweet and home-like strain:
And the tartan clove the turban,
   As the Goomtee cleaves the plain.

Dear to the corn-land reaper
  And plaided mountaineer,
To the cottage and the castle
  The piper's song is dear.
Sweet sounds the Gaelic pibroch
  O'er mountain, glen and glade;
But the sweetest of all music
  The Pipes at Lucknow played!

*John Greenleaf Whittier*

## TRAGIC TALES

### THE WRECK OF THE HESPERUS

It was the schooner Hesperus,
　　That sailed the wintry sea;
And the skipper had taken his little daughter,
　　To bear him company.

Blue were her eyes as the fairy-flax,
　　Her cheeks like the dawn of day,
And her bosom white as the hawthorn buds
　　That ope in the month of May.

The skipper he stood beside the helm,
　　His pipe was in his mouth,
And he watched how the veering flaw did blow
　　The smoke now west, now south.

Then up and spake an old sailor,
　　Had sailed the Spanish Main,
"I pray thee, put into yonder port,
　　For I fear a hurricane.

"Last night the moon had a golden ring,
　　And to-night no moon we see!"
The skipper he blew a whiff from his pipe,
　　And a scornful laugh laughed he.

Colder and louder blew the wind,
　　A gale from the north-east,
The snow fell hissing in the brine,
　　And the billows frothed like yeast.

Down came the storm, and smote amain
   The vessel in its strength;
She shuddered and paused, like a frighted steed,
   Then leaped her cable's length.

"Come hither! come hither! my little daughter,
   And do not tremble so;
For I can weather the roughest gale
   That ever wind did blow."

He wrapped her warm in his seaman's coat
   Against the stinging blast;
He cut a rope from a broken spar,
   And bound her to the mast.

"O father! I hear the church-bells ring,
   O say, what may it be?"
"'Tis a fog-bell on a rock-bound coast!"—
   And he steered for the open sea.

"O father! I hear the sound of guns,
   O say, what may it be?"
"Some ship in distress, that cannot live
   In such an angry sea!"

"O father! I see a gleaming light,
   O say, what may it be?"
But the father answered never a word,
   A frozen corpse was he.

Lashed to the helm, all stiff and stark,
   With his face turned to the skies,
The lantern gleamed through the gleaming snow
   On his fixed and glassy eyes.

Then the maiden clasped her hands and prayed
   That savèd she might be;
And she thought of Christ, who stilled the wave
   On the Lake of Galilee.

And fast through the midnight dark and drear,
   Through the whistling sleet and snow,
Like a sheeted ghost, the vessel swept
   Towards the reef of Norman's Woe.

And ever the fitful gusts between
   A sound came from the land;
It was the sound of the trampling surf
   On the rocks and the hard sea-sand.

The breakers were right beneath her bows,
   She drifted a dreary wreck,
And a whooping billow swept the crew
   Like icicles from her deck.

She struck where the white and fleecy waves
   Looked soft as carded wool,
But the cruel rocks, they gored her side
   Like the horns of an angry bull.

Her rattling shrouds, all sheathed in ice,
   With the masts, went by the board;
Like a vessel of glass she stove and sank;
   Ho! ho! the breakers roared!

At daybreak on the bleak sea-beach
   A fisherman stood aghast,
To see the form of a maiden fair
   Lashed close to a drifting mast,

The salt sea was frozen on her breast,
   The salt tears in her eyes;
And he saw her hair, like the brown sea-weed,
   On the billows fall and rise.

Such was the wreck of the Hesperus,
   In the midnight and the snow!
Christ save us all from a death like this,
   On the reef of Norman's Woe!

*Henry Wadsworth Longfellow*

### THE THREE FISHERS

THREE fishers went sailing away to the West,
   Away to the West as the sun went down;
Each thought on the woman who loved him the
   best,
   And the children stood watching them out of
   the town;
For men must work, and women must weep,
And there's little to earn, and many to keep,
   Though the harbour bar be moaning.

Three wives sat up in the lighthouse tower,
   And they trimmed the lamps as the sun went
   down;
They looked at the squall, and they looked at the
   shower,
   And the night-rack came rolling up ragged and
   brown;

But men must work, and women must weep,
Though storms be sudden, and waters deep,
   And the harbour bar be moaning.

Three corpses lay out on the shining sands,
   In the morning gleam, as the tide went down,
And the women are weeping and wringing their
     hands
   For those who will never come back to the
     town;
For men must work, and women must weep,
And the sooner it's over, the sooner to sleep;
   And good-bye to the bar and its moaning.

*Charles Kingsley*


### THE LOWLANDS OF HOLLAND

My love he built a bonny ship, and set her on
   the sea,
Wi' seven score good mariners to bear her
   companie.
There's three score is sunk, and three score dead
   at sea,
And the Lowlands of Holland hae twined my
   love and me.

"My love he built another ship, and set her on
   the main,
And nane but twenty mariners for to bring her
   hame;

But the weary wind began to rise, and the sea
    began to rout,
My love then and his bonny ship turned wither-
    shins about.

"There shall neither coif come on my head, nor
    kaim come in my hair,
There shall neither coal nor candlelight shine in
    my bower mair;
Nor will I love another ane until the day I dee,
For I never loved a love but ane, and he's drowned
    in the sea."

"O haud your tongue, my daughter dear, be still
    and be content;
There are mair lads in Galloway, ye needna sair
    lament."
"O there is nane in Galloway, there's nane at a'
    for me,
For I never loved a love but ane, and he's drowned
    in the sea."

*Anonymous*

### LORD RANDAL

"O where hae ye been, Lord Randal, my son?
O where hae ye been, my handsome young man?"
"I hae been to the wild wood; mother, make my
    bed soon,
For I'm weary wi' hunting, and fain wad lie
    down."

"Where gat ye your dinner, Lord Randal, my
    son?
Where gat ye your dinner, my handsome young
    man?"
"I dined wi' my true-love; mother, make my bed
    soon,
For I'm weary wi' hunting, and fain wad lie
    down."

"What gat ye to your dinner, Lord Randal, my
    son?
What gat ye to your dinner, my handsome young
    man?"
"I gat eels boiled in broo; mother, make my bed
    soon,
For I'm weary wi' hunting, and fain wad lie
    down."

"What became of your bloodhounds, Lord Randal,
    my son?
What became of your bloodhounds, my handsome
    young man?"
"Oh, they swelled and they died; mother, make
    my bed soon,
For I'm weary wi' hunting, and fain wad lie
    down."

"O I fear ye are poisoned, Lord Randal, my son!
O I fear ye are poisoned, my handsome young
    man?"
"O yes! I am poisoned; mother, make my bed
    soon,
For I'm sick at the heart, and I fain wad lie down."

*Anonymous*

### THE HIGH-BORN LADYE

In vain all the Knights of the Underwald woo'd
    her,
  Though brightest of maidens, the proudest was
    she;
Brave chieftains they sought, and young minstrels
    they sued her,
  But worthy were none of the high-born Ladye.

"Whomsoever I wed," said this maid, so excelling,
  "That Knight must the conqu'ror of conquerors
    be;
He must place me in halls fit for monarchs to
    dwell in—
  None else shall be Lord of the high-born
    Ladye!"

Thus spoke the proud damsel, with scorn looking
    round her,
  On Knights and on Nobles of highest degree,
Who humbly and hopelessly left as they found her
  And worshipp'd at distance the high-born
    Ladye.

At length came a Knight from a far land to woo
    her,
  With plumes on his helm like the foam of the
    sea;
His vizor was down—but, with voice that thrill'd
    through her,
  He whisper'd his vows to the high-born Ladye.

"Proud maiden! I come with high spousals to
    grace thee,
  In me the great conqu'ror of conquerors
    see;
Enthroned in a hall fit for monarchs I'll place
    thee,
  And mine thou'rt for ever, thou high-born
    Ladye!"

The maiden she smil'd, and in jewels array'd
    her,
  Of thrones and tiaras already dreamt she,
And proud was the step, as her bridegroom con-
    vey'd her
  In pomp to his home, of that high-born Ladye.

"But whither," she, starting, exclaims, "have you
    led me?
  Here's nought but a tomb and a dark cypress-
    tree;
Is *this* the bright palace in which thou wouldst wed
    me?"
  With scorn in her glance, said the high-born
    Ladye.

" 'Tis the home," he replied, "of earth's loftiest
    creatures"—
  Then lifted his helm for the fair one to see,
But she sunk on the ground—'twas a skeleton's
    features,
  And Death was the Lord of the high-born
    Ladye!

                              *Thomas Moore*

## YOUNG WATERS

ABOUT Yule, when the wind blew cool,
    And the round tables began,
Ah! there is come to our King's court
    Many a well-favoured man.

The Queen looked o'er the castle wall,
    Beheld both dale and down,
And then she saw Young Waters
    Come riding to the town.

His footmen they did run before,
    His horsemen rode behind;
A mantle of the burning gold
    Did keep him from the wind.

Out then spake a wily lord,
    Unto the Queen said he,
"Oh, tell me who's the fairest face
    Rides in the company?"

"Oh, I've seen lord, and I've seen laird,
    And knights of high degree,
But a fairer face than Young Waters'
    Mine eyes did never see."

Out then spake the jealous King
    (And an angry man was he):
"Oh, if he had been twice as fair,
    You might have excepted me."

"You're neither laird nor lord," she says,
    "But the King that wears the crown;
There is not a knight in fair Scotland
    But to thee must bow down."

For all that she could do or say,
    Appeased he would not be;
But for the words which she had said,
    Young Waters he must dee.

They have ta'en Young Waters,
    And put fetters to his feet;
They have ta'en Young Waters,
    And thrown him in dungeon deep.

"Oft I have ridden thro' Stirling town
    In the wind but and the wet;
But I ne'er rode thro' Stirling town
    With fetters at my feet.

"Oft have I ridden through Stirling town
    In the wind but and the rain;
But I ne'er rode thro' Stirling town
    Ne'er to return again."

They have ta'en to the heiding-hill
    His young son in the cradle,
And they have ta'en to the heiding-hill
    His horse but and his saddle.

They have ta'en to the heiding-hill
    His lady fair to see;
And for the words the Queen had spoke,
    Young Waters he did dee.

                                    *Anonymous*

## SHAMEFUL DEATH

THERE were four of us about that bed;
  The mass-priest knelt at the side,
I and his mother stood at the head,
  Over his feet lay the bride;
We were quite sure that he was dead,
  Though his eyes were open wide.

He did not die in the night,
  He did not die in the day,
But in the morning twilight
  His spirit passed away,
When neither sun nor moon was bright,
  And the trees were merely grey.

He was not slain with the sword,
  Knight's axe, or the knightly spear,
Yet spoke he never a word
  After he came in here;
I cut away the cord
  From the neck of my brother dear.

He did not strike one blow,
  For the recreants came behind,
In a place where the hornbeams grow,
  A path right hard to find,
For the hornbeam boughs swing so,
  That the twilight makes it blind.

They lighted a great torch then,
  When his arms were pinioned fast;
Sir John the Knight of the Fen,
  Sir Guy of the Dolorous Blast,

With knights threescore and ten,
  Hung brave Lord Hugh at last.

I am threescore and ten,
  And my hair is all turned grey,
But I met Sir John of the Fen
  Long ago on a summer day,
And am glad to think of the moment when
  I took his life away.

I am threescore and ten,
  And my strength is mostly passed,
But long ago I and my men,
  When the sky was overcast,
And the smoke rolled over the reeds of the
    fen,
  Slew Guy of the Dolorous Blast.

And now, knights, all of you,
  I pray you, pray for Sir Hugh,
A good knight and a true,
  And for Alice, his wife, pray too.

                        *William Morris*

# *HAPPY ENDINGS*

## GREEN BROOM

THERE was an old man lived out in the wood,
    His trade was a-cutting of Broom, green Broom:
He had but one son without thrift, without good,
    Who lay in his bed till 'twas noon, bright noon.

The old man awoke, one morning and spoke,
    He swore he would fire the room, that room,
If his John would not rise and open his eyes,
    And away to the wood to cut Broom, green
      Broom.

So Johnny arose, and he slipped on his clothes,
    And away to the wood to cut Broom, green
      Broom,
He sharpened his knives, for once he contrives
    To cut a great bundle of Broom, green Broom.

When Johnny passed under a lady's fine house,
    Passed under a lady's fine room, fine room,
She called to her maid, "Go fetch me," she said,
    "Go fetch me the boy that sells Broom, green
      Broom."

When Johnny came in to the lady's fine house,
    And stood in the lady's fine room, fine room;
"Young Johnny," she said, "will you give up
    your trade,
    And marry a lady in bloom, full bloom?"

Johnny gave his consent, and to church they both
    went,
  And he wedded the lady in bloom, full bloom.
At market and fair, all folks do declare,
  There is none like the Boy that sold Broom,
    green Broom.

*Anonymous*


## JOCK OF HAZELDEAN

"WHY weep ye by the tide, ladie?
  Why weep ye by the tide?
I'll wed ye to my youngest son,
  And ye sall be his bride;
And ye sall be his bride, ladie,
  Sae comely to be seen"—
But aye she loot the tears down fa'
  For Jock of Hazeldean.

"Now let this wilfu' grief be done,
  And dry that cheek so pale;
Young Frank is chief of Errington,
  And lord of Langley-dale;
His step is first in peaceful ha',
  His sword in battle keen"—
But aye she loot the tears down fa'
  For Jock of Hazeldean.

"A chain of gold ye sall not lack,
  Nor braid to bind your hair;
Nor mettled hound, nor managed hawk,
  Nor palfrey fresh and fair;

And you, the foremost o' them a',
   Sall ride our forest queen"—
But aye she loot the tears down fa'
   For Jock of Hazeldean.

The kirk was decked at morning-tide,
   The tapers glimmered fair;
The priest and bridegroom wait the bride,
   And dame and knight are there.
They sought her baith by bower and ha';
   The ladie was not seen!
She's o'er the Border, and awa'
   Wi' Jock of Hazeldean.

*Sir Walter Scott*

### ALLEN-A-DALE

ALLEN-A-DALE has no fagot for burning,
Allen-a-Dale has no furrow for turning,
Allen-a-Dale has no fleece for the spinning,
Yet Allen-a-Dale has red gold for the winning!
Come, read me my riddle! come, hearken my
   tale!
And tell me the craft of bold Allen-a-Dale.

The Baron of Ravensworth prances in pride,
And he views his domains upon Arkindale side,
The mere for his net, and the land for his game,
The chase for the wild, and the park for the
   tame,

Yet the fish of the lake and the deer of the vale
Are less free to Lord Dacre than Allen-a-Dale!

Allen-a-Dale was ne'er belted a knight,
Though his spear be as sharp, and his blade be as
    bright;
Allen-a-Dale is no baron or lord,
Yet twenty tall yeomen will draw at his word;
And the best of our nobles his bonnet will vail,
Who at Rere-cross on Stanmore meets Allen-a-
    Dale.

Allen-a-Dale to his wooing is come;
The mother, she asked of his household and home;
"Though the castle of Richmond stands fair on
    the hill,
My hall," quoth bold Allen, "shows gallanter still;
'Tis the blue vault of heaven, with its crescent so
    pale,
And with all its bright spangles!" said Allen-a-
    Dale.

The father was steel, and the mother was stone;
They lifted the latch, and they bade him be
    gone;
But loud, on the morrow, their wail and their
    cry:
He had laughed on the lass with his bonny black
    eye;
And she fled to the forest to hear a love-tale,
And the youth it was told by was Allen-a-Dale!

*Sir Walter Scott*

### THE BAILIFF'S DAUGHTER OF ISLINGTON

There was a youth, a well-belovèd youth,
　　And he was a squire's son;
He loved the bailiff's daughter dear,
　　That lived in Islington.


Yet she was coy and would not believe
　　That he did love her so,
No, nor at any time would she
　　Any countenance to him show.


But when his friends did understand
　　His fond and foolish mind,
They sent him up to fair London
　　An apprentice for to bind.


And when he had been seven long years,
　　And never his love could see,
Many a tear have I shed for her sake
　　When she little thought of me.


Then all the maids of Islington
　　Went forth to sport and play;
All but the bailiff's daughter dear;
　　She secretly stole away.


She pullèd off her gown of green
　　And put on ragged attire,
And to fair London she would go,
　　Her true love to enquire.

And as she went along the high road,
    The weather being hot and dry,
She sat her down upon a green bank,
    And her true-love came riding by.

She started up, with a colour so red,
    Catching hold of his bridle-rein;
"One penny, one penny, kind sir," she said,
    "Will ease me of much pain."

"Before I give you one penny, sweetheart,
    Pray tell me where you were born."
"At Islington, kind sir," said she,
    "Where I have had many a scorn."

"I prithee, sweetheart, then tell to me,
    O tell me, whether you know
The bailiff's daughter of Islington."
    "She is dead, sir, long ago."

"If she be dead, then take my horse,
    My saddle and bridle also;
For I will unto some far countree,
    Where no man shall me know."

" O stay, O stay, thou goodly youth,
    She standeth by thy side;
She is here alive, she is not dead,
    And ready to be thy bride."

" O farewell grief, and welcome joy,
    Ten thousand times therefore;
For now I have found mine own true-love
    Whom I thought I should never see more."

*Anonymous*

### THE HORN OF EGREMONT CASTLE

ERE the Brothers through the gateway
Issued forth with old and young,
To the Horn Sir Eustace pointed
Which for ages there had hung.
Horn it was which none could sound,
No one upon living ground,
Save He who came as rightful Heir
To Egremont's Domains and Castle fair.

Heirs from times of earliest record
Had the House of Lucie born,
Who of right had held the Lordship
Claimed by proof upon the Horn:
Each at the appointed hour
Tried the Horn,—it owned his power;
He was acknowledged: and the blast,
Which good Sir Eustace sounded, was the last.

With his lance Sir Eustace pointed,
And to Hubert thus said he,
"What I speak this Horn shall witness
For thy better memory.
Hear, then, and neglect me not!
At this time, and on this spot,
The words are uttered from my heart,
As my last earnest prayer ere we depart.

"On good service we are going
Life to risk by sea and land,
In which course if Christ our Saviour
Do my sinful soul demand,

Hither come thou back straightway,
Hubert, if alive that day;
Return, and sound the Horn, that we
May have a living House still left in thee!"

"Fear not," quickly answered Hubert;
"As I am thy Father's son,
What thou askest, noble Brother,
With God's favour shall be done."
So were both right well content:
Forth they from the Castle went,
And at the head of their Array
To Palestine the Brothers took their way.

Side by side they fought (the Lucies
Were a line for valour famed),
And where'er their strokes alighted,
There the Saracens were tamed.
Whence, then, could it come—the thought—
By what evil spirit brought?
Oh! can a brave Man wish to take
His brother's life, for Lands' and Castle's
    sake?

"Sir!" the Ruffians said to Hubert,
"Deep he lies in Jordan flood."
Stricken by this ill assurance,
Pale and trembling Hubert stood.
"Take your earnings."—Oh! that I
Could have *seen* my Brother die!
It was a pang that vexed him then;
And oft returned, again, and yet again.

Months passed on, and no Sir Eustace!
Nor of him were tidings heard;
Wherefore, bold as day, the Murderer
Back again to England steered.
To his Castle Hubert sped;
Nothing has he now to dread.
But silent and by stealth he came,
And at an hour which nobody could name.

None could tell if it were night-time,
Night or day, at even or morn;
No one's eye had seen him enter,
No one's ear had heard the Horn.
But bold Hubert lives in glee:
Months and years went smilingly;
With plenty was his table spread;
And bright the Lady is who shares his
    bed.

Likewise he had sons and daughters;
And, as good men do, he sate
At his board by these surrounded,
Flourishing in fair estate.
And while thus in open day
Once he sate, as old books say,
A blast was uttered from the Horn,
Where by the Castle-gate it hung forlorn.

'Tis the breath of good Sir Eustace!
He is come to claim his right:
Ancient castle, woods, and mountains
Hear the challenge with delight.

Hubert! though the blast be blown
He is helpless and alone:
Thou hast a dungeon, speak the word!
And there he may be lodged, and thou be Lord.

Speak!—astounded Hubert cannot;
And, if power to speak he had,
All are daunted, all the household
Smitten to the heart, and sad.
'Tis Sir Eustace; if it be
Living man, it must be he!
Thus Hubert thought in his dismay,
And by a postern-gate he slunk away.

Long, and long was he unheard of:
To his Brother then he came,
Made confession, asked forgiveness,
Asked it by a brother's name,
And by all the saints in heaven;
And of Eustace was forgiven:
Then in a convent went to hide
His melancholy head, and there he died.

But Sir Eustace, whom good angels
Had preserved from murderers' hands,
And from Pagan chains had rescued,
Lived with honour on his lands.
Sons he had, saw sons of theirs:
And through ages, heirs of heirs,
A long posterity renowned,
Sounded the Horn which they alone could
    sound.

*William Wordsworth*

## LADY CLARE

IT was the time when lilies blow,
   And clouds are highest up in air,
Lord Ronald brought a lily-white doe
   To give his cousin, Lady Clare.

I trow they did not part in scorn:
   Lovers long-betroth'd were they:
They two will wed the morrow morn;
   God's blessing on the day!

"He does not love me for my birth,
   Nor for my lands so broad and fair;
He loves me for my own true worth,
   And that is well," said Lady Clare.

In there came old Alice the nurse,
   Said, "Who was this that went from thee?"
"It was my cousin," said Lady Clare,
   "To-morrow he weds with me."

"O God be thank'd!" said Alice the nurse,
   "That all comes round so just and fair:
Lord Ronald is heir of all your lands,
   And you are not the Lady Clare."

"Are ye out of your mind, my nurse, my
     nurse?"
   Said Lady Clare, "that ye speak so wild?"
"As God's above," said Alice the nurse,
   "I speak the truth: you are my child.

"The old Earl's daughter died at my breast;
   I speak the truth, as I live by bread!

I buried her like my own sweet child,
  And put my child in her stead."

"Falsely, falsely, have ye done,
  O mother," she said, "if this be true,
To keep the best man under the sun
  So many years from his due."

"Nay now, my child," said Alice the nurse,
  "But keep the secret for your life,
And all you have will be Lord Ronald's,
  When you are man and wife."

"If I'm a beggar born," she said,
  "I will speak out, for I dare not lie.
Pull off, pull off, the brooch of gold,
  And fling the diamond necklace by."

"Nay now, my child," said Alice the nurse,
  "But keep the secret all ye can."
She said "Not so: but I will know
  If there be any faith in man."

"Nay now, what faith?" said Alice the nurse,
  "The man will cleave unto his right."
"And he shall have it," the lady replied,
  "Tho' I should die to-night."

"Yet give one kiss to your mother dear!
  Alas, my child, I sinn'd for thee."
"O mother, mother, mother," she said,
  "So strange it seems to me.

"Yet here's a kiss for my mother dear,
  My mother dear, if this be so,
And lay your hand upon my head,
  And bless me, mother, ere I go."

She clad herself in a russet gown,
   She was no longer Lady Clare:
She went by dale, and she went by down,
   With a single rose in her hair.

The lily-white doe Lord Ronald had brought
   Leapt up from where she lay,
Dropt her head in the maiden's hand,
   And follow'd her all the way.

Down stept Lord Ronald from his tower:
   "O Lady Clare, you shame your worth!
Why come you drest like a village maid,
   That are the flower of the earth?"

"If I come drest like a village maid,
   I am but as my fortunes are:
I am a beggar born," she said,
   "And not the Lady Clare."

"Play me no tricks," said Lord Ronald,
   "For I am yours in word and in deed.
Play me no tricks," said Lord Ronald,
   "Your riddle is hard to read."

O and proudly stood she up!
   Her heart within her did not fail:
She look'd into Lord Ronald's eyes,
   And told him all her nurse's tale.

He laugh'd a laugh of merry scorn:
   He turn'd and kiss'd her where she stood:
"If you are not the heiress born,
   And I," said he, "the next in blood—

"If you are not the heiress born,
  And I," said he, "the lawful heir,
We two will wed to-morrow morn,
  And you shall still be Lady Clare."

*Alfred, Lord Tennyson*


### HYND HORN

HYND HORN'S bound, love, and Hynd Horn's free,
  *With a hey lillelu, and a how lo lan;*
Where was ye born, or in what countrie?
  *And the birk and the broom blows bonnie.*

"In good greenwood, there I was born,
And all my forbears me beforn.

"O seven long years I served the King,
And as for wages I never gat nane;

"But ae sight o' his ae daughter.
And that was through an auger-bore."

Seven long years he served the King,
And it's a' for the sake of his daughter Jean.

The King an angry man was he;
He sent young Hynd Horn to the sea.

He's gi'en his love a silver wand
Wi' seven silver laverocks sittin' thereon.

She's gi'en to him a gay gold ring
Wi' seven bright diamonds set therein.

"As lang's these diamonds keep their hue,
Ye'll know I am a lover true;

"But when the ring turns pale and wan,
Ye may ken that I love anither man."

He hoist up sails and awa' sailed he
Till that he came to a foreign countrie.

One day as he looked his ring upon,
He saw the diamonds pale and wan.

He's left the seas and he's come to the land,
And the first that he met was an auld beggar-man.

"What news, what news? thou auld beggar-man,
For it's seven years sin I've seen land."

"No news," said the beggar, "no news at a',
But there is a wedding in the King's ha'.

"But there is a wedding in the King's ha',
That has halden these forty days and twa."

"Cast off, cast off thy auld beggar weed,
And I'll gi'e thee my gude grey steed;

"And lend to me your wig o' hair
To cover mine, because it is fair."

"My begging weed is na for thee,
Your riding steed is na for me."

But part by right and part by wrang
Hynd Horn has changed wi' the beggar-man.

The auld beggar-man was bound for to ride,
But young Hynd Horn was bound for the
    bride.

When he·came to the King's gate,
He sought a drink for Hynd Horn's sake.

The bride came trippin' down the stair,
Wi' the scales o' red gowd in her hair;

Wi' a cup o' the red wine in her hand,
And that she gae to the auld beggar-man.

Out o' the cup he drank the wine,
And into the cup he dropt the ring.

"O got ye this by sea or land?
Or got ye it of a dead man's hand?"

"I got it na by sea nor land,
But I got it, madam, of your own hand."

"O I'll cast off my gowns o' brown,
And beg with you frae town to town.

"O I'll cast off my gowns o' red,
And I'll beg wi' you to win my bread.

"O I'll take the scales o' gowd frae my hair,
And I'll follow you for evermair."

She has cast awa' the brown and the red,
And she's followed him to beg her bread.

She has ta'en the scales o' gowd frae her hair
And she's followed him for evermair.

But atween the kitchen and the ha'
He has let his cloutie cloak down fa'.

And the red gowd shinèd over him a',
*With a hey lillelu, and a how lo lan;*
And the bride frae the bridegroom was stown awa'
*And the birk and the broom blows bonnie.*

*Anonymous*

N

## ENGLAND, MY ENGLAND

WHAT have I done for you,
  England, my England?
What is there I would not do,
  England, my own?
With your glorious eyes austere,
As the Lord were walking near,
Whispering terrible things and dear
    As the Song on your bugles blown,
    England—
    Round the world on your bugles
    blown!

Where shall the watchful Sun,
  England, my England,
Match the master-work you've done,
  England, my own?
When shall he rejoice agen
Such a breed of mighty men
As come forward, one to ten,
    To the Song on your bugles blown,
    England—
    Down the years on your bugles
    blown?

Ever the faith endures,
  England, my England:—
"Take and break us: we are yours,
  England, my own!

Life is good, and joy runs high
Between English earth and sky:
Death is death: but we shall die
    To the Song on your bugles blown,
    England—
    To the stars on your bugles
      blown!"


They call you proud and hard,
  England, my England:
You with worlds to watch and ward,
  England, my own!
You whose mailed hand keeps the keys
Of such teeming destinies,
You could know nor dread nor ease
    Were the Song on your bugles blown,
    England,
    Round the Pit on your bugles
      blown!


Mother of Ships whose might,
  England, my England,
Is the fierce old Sea's delight,
  England, my own,
Chosen daughter of the Lord,
Spouse-in-Chief of the ancient Sword,
There's the menace of the Word
    In the Song on your bugles blown,
    England—
    Out of heaven on your bugles blown!

*W. E. Henley*

### THE ENGLISHMAN

I MET a sailor in the woods,
 A silver ring wore he,
His hair hung black, his eyes shone blue,
 And thus he said to me:

"What country, say, of this round earth,
 What shore of what salt sea,
Be this, my son, I wander in,
 And looks so strange to me?"

Says I, "Oh foreign sailorman,
 In England now you be,
This is her wood, and this her sky,
 And that her roaring sea."

He lifts his voice yet louder,
 "What smell be this," says he,
"My nose on the sharp morning air
 Snuffs up so greedily?"

Says I, "It is wild roses
 Do smell so winsomely,
And winy briar too," says I,
 "That in these thickets be."

"And oh!" says he, "what leetle bird
 Is singing in yon high tree,
So every shrill and long-drawn note
 Like bubbles breaks in me?"

Says I, "It is the mavis
   That perches in the tree
And sings so shrill, and sings so sweet,
   When dawn comes up the sea."

At which he fell a-musing,
   And fixed his eye on me,
As one alone 'twixt light and dark
   A spirit thinks to see.

"England!" he whispers soft and harsh,
   "England!" repeated he,
"And briar, and rose, and mavis
   A-singing in yon high tree.

"Ye speak me true, my leetle son,
   So—so, it came to me,
A-drifting landwards on a spar,
   And grey dawn on the sea.

"Ay, ay; I could not be mistook;
   I knew them leafy trees,
I knew that land so witcherie sweet,
   And that old noise of seas.

"Though here I've sailed a score of years,
   And heard 'em, dream or wake,
Lap small and hollow 'gainst my cheek,
   On sand and coral break;

" 'Yet now,' my leetle son, says I,
   A-drifting on the wave,
'That land I see so safe and green
   Is England, I believe.

" 'And that there wood is English wood,
   And this here cruel sea

The self-same old blue ocean
   Years gone remembers me.

" 'A-sitting with my bread and butter
   Down ahind yon chitterin' mill;
And this same Marinere'—(that's me),
   'Is that same leetle Will!—

" 'That very same wee leetle Will
   Eating his bread and butter there,
A-looking on the broad blue sea
   Betwixt his yaller hair!'

"And here be I, my son, throwed up
   Like corpses from the sea,
Ships, stars, winds, tempests, pirates past,
   Yet leetle Will I be!"

He said no more, that sailorman,
   But in a reverie
Stared, like the figure of a ship
   With painted eyes, to sea.

               *Walter de la Mare*


### THE SONG OF THE BOW

WHAT of the bow?
   The bow was made in England:
Of true wood, of yew-wood,
   The wood of English bows;
      So men who are free
      Love the old yew-tree
And the land where the yew-tree grows.

What of the cord?
   The cord was made in England:
A rough cord, a tough cord,
   A cord that bowmen love;
      And so we will sing
      Of the hempen string,
And the land where the cord was wove.

What of the shaft?
   The shaft was cut in England:
A long shaft, a strong shaft,
   Barbed and trim and true;
      So we'll drink all together
      To the grey goose-feather,
And the land where the grey goose flew.

What of the mark?
   Ah, seek it not in England:
A bold mark, our old mark
   Is waiting over-sea.
      When the strings harp in chorus,
      And the lion flag is o'er us,
It is there that our mark will be.

What of the men?
   The men were bred in England.
The bowmen—the yeomen,
   The lads of dale and fell.
      Here's to you—and to you
      To the hearts that are true,
And the land where the true hearts dwell.

*Sir Arthur Conan Doyle*

## SHERWOOD

Sherwood in the twilight, is Robin Hood awake?
Grey and ghostly shadows are gliding through the
brake;
Shadows of the dappled deer, dreaming of the
morn,
Dreaming of a shadowy man that winds a
shadowy horn.

Robin Hood is here again: all his merry thieves
Hear a ghostly bugle-note shivering through the
leaves,
Calling as he used to call, faint and far away,
In Sherwood, in Sherwood, about the break of day.

Merry, merry England has kissed the lips of June:
All the wings of fairyland were here beneath the
moon
Like a flight of rose-leaves fluttering in a mist
Of opal and ruby and pearl and amethyst.

Merry, merry England is waking as of old,
With eyes of blither hazel and hair of brighter
gold:
For Robin Hood is here again beneath the burst-
ing spray
In Sherwood, in Sherwood, about the break of day.

Love is in the greenwood building him a house
Of wild rose and hawthorn and honeysuckle
boughs.
Love is in the greenwood, dawn is in the skies;
And Marian is waiting with a glory in her eyes.

Hark! The dazzled laverock climbs the golden
steep:
Marian is waiting: Is Robin Hood asleep?
Round the fairy grass-rings frolic elf and fay
In Sherwood, in Sherwood, about the break of
day.

Oberon, Oberon, rake away the gold,
Rake away the red leaves, roll away the mould,
Rake away the gold leaves, roll away the red,
And wake Will Scarlett from his leafy forest
bed.

Friar Tuck and Little John are riding down
together
With quarter-staff and drinking-can and grey
goose-feather.
The dead are coming back again; the years are
rolled away
In Sherwood, in Sherwood, about the break of
day.

Softly over Sherwood the south wind blows;
All the heart of England hid in every rose
Hears across the greenwood the sunny whisper
leap,
Sherwood in the red dawn, is Robin Hood asleep?

Hark, the voice of England wakes him as of old
And, shattering the silence with a cry of brighter
gold,
Bugles in the greenwood echo from the steep,
*Sherwood in the red dawn, is Robin Hood asleep?*

Where the deer are gliding down the shadowy
    glen
All across the glades of fern he calls his merry men;
Doublets of the Lincoln green glancing through
    the may
In Sherwood, in Sherwood, about the break of
    day;

Calls them and they answer: from aisles of oak
    and ash
Rings the *Follow! Follow!* and the boughs begin
    to crash;
The ferns begin to flutter and the flowers begin
    to fly;
And through the crimson dawning the robber
    band goes by.

*Robin! Robin! Robin!* All his merry thieves
Answer as the bugle-note shivers through the
    leaves:
Calling as he used to call, faint and far away,
In Sherwood, in Sherwood, about the break of day.

*Alfred Noyes*

### DRAKE'S DRUM

Drake he's in his hammock an' a thousand mile
    away,
    (Capten, art tha sleepin' there below?),
Slung atween the round shot in Nombre Dios Bay,
    An' dreamin' arl the time o' Plymouth Hoe.

Yarnder lumes the Island, yarnder lie the ships,
  Wi' sailor-lads a-dancin' heel-an'-toe,
An' the shore-lights flashin', and the night-tide
    dashin',
  He sees et arl so plainly as he saw et long
    ago.

Drake he was a Devon man, an' rüled the Devon
    seas,
  (Capten, art tha sleepin' there below?),
Rovin' tho' his death fell, he went wi' heart at
    ease,
  An' dreamin' arl the time o' Plymouth Hoe.
"Take my drum to England, hang et by the
    shore,
  Strike et when your powder's runnin' low;
If the Dons sight Devon, I'll quit the port o'
    Heaven,
  An' drum them up the Channel as we drummed
    them long ago."

Drake he's in his hammock till the great Armadas
    come,
  (Capten, art tha sleepin' there below?),
Slung atween the round shot, listenin' for the
    drum,
  An' dreamin' arl the time o' Plymouth Hoe.
Call him on the deep sea, call him up the Sound,
  Call him when ye sail to meet the foe;
Where the old trade's plyin' an' the old flag flyin'
  They shall find him ware an' wakin', as they
    found him long ago!

*Sir Henry Newbolt*

### A BALLAD OF THE FLEET

At Flores in the Azores Sir Richard Grenville
    lay,
And a pinnace, like a fluttered bird, came flying
    from far away:
"Spanish ships of war at sea! we have sighted
    fifty-three!"
Then sware Lord Thomas Howard: " 'Fore God
    I am no coward;
But I cannot meet them here, for my ships are
    out of gear,
And the half my men are sick.  I must fly, but
    follow quick.
We are six ships of the line;  can we fight with
    fifty-three?"

Then spake Sir Richard Grenville: "I know you
    are no coward;
You fly them for a moment to fight with them
    again.
But I've ninety men and more that are lying sick
    ashore.
I should count myself the coward if I left them,
    my Lord Howard,
To these Inquisition dogs and the devildoms of
    Spain."

So Lord Howard passed away with five ships of
    war that day,
Till he melted like a cloud in the silent summer
    heaven;

But Sir Richard bore in hand all his sick men from
    the land
Very carefully and slow,
Men of Bideford in Devon,
And we laid them on the ballast down below;
For we brought them all aboard,
And they blest him in their pain, that they were
    not left to Spain,
To the thumbscrew and the stake, for the glory
    of the Lord.

He had only a hundred seamen to work the ship
    and to fight,
And he sailed away from Flores till the Spaniard
    came in sight,
With his huge sea-castles heaving upon the
    weather bow.
"Shall we fight or shall we fly?
Good Sir Richard, tell us now,
For to fight is but to die!
There'll be little of us left by the time this sun be
    set."
And Sir Richard said again: "We be all good
    English men.
Let us bang these dogs of Seville, the children of
    the devil,
For I never turned my back upon Don or devil
    yet."

Sir Richard spoke and he laughed, and we roared
    a hurrah, and so
The little *Revenge* ran on sheer into the heart of
    the foe,

With her hundred fighters on deck, and her
  ninety sick below;
For half of their fleet to the right and half to the
  left were seen,
And the little *Revenge* ran on through the long
  sea-lane between.


Thousands of their soldiers looked down from
  their decks and laughed,
Thousands of their seamen made mock at the
  mad little craft
Running on and on, till delayed
By their mountain-like *San Philip* that, of fifteen
  hundred tons,
And up-shadowing high above us with her yawning
  tiers of guns,
Took the breath from our sails, and we stayed.


And while now the great *San Philip* hung above us
  like a cloud
Whence the thunderbolt will fall
Long and loud,
Four galleons drew away
From the Spanish fleet that day,
And two upon the larboard and two upon the
  starboard lay,
And the battle-thunder broke from them all.


But anon the great *San Philip*, she bethought herself and went,
Having that within her womb that had left her
  ill content;

And the rest they came aboard us, and they fought
    us hand to hand,
For a dozen times they came with their pikes and
    musqueteers,
And a dozen times we shook 'em off as a dog that
    shakes his ears
When he leaps from the water to the land.

·And the sun went down, and the stars came out
    far over the summer sea,
But never a moment ceased the fight of the one
    and the fifty-three.
Ship after ship, the whole night long, their high-
    built galleons came,
Ship after ship, the whole night long, with her
    battle-thunder and flame;
Ship after ship, the whole night long, drew back
    with her dead and her shame.
For some were sunk and many were shattered,
    and so could fight us no more—
God of battles, was ever a battle like this in the
    world before?

For he said, "Fight on! fight on!"
Though his vessel was all but a wreck;
And it chanced that, when half of the short
    summer night was gone,
With a grisly wound to be dressed he had left the
    deck,
But a bullet struck him that was dressing it
    suddenly dead,
And himself he was wounded again in the side
    and the head,
And he said, "Fight on! fight on!"

And the night went down, and the sun smiled out
    far over the summer sea,
And the Spanish fleet with broken sides lay round
    us all in a ring;
But they dared not touch us again, for they feared
    that we still could sting,
So they watched what the end would be.
And we had not fought them in vain,
But in perilous plight were we,
Seeing forty of our poor hundred were slain,
And half of the rest of us maimed for life
In the crash of the cannonades and the desperate
    strife;
And the sick men down in the hold were most of
    them stark and cold,


And the pikes were all broken or bent, and the
    powder was all of it spent;
And the masts and the rigging were lying over
    the side;
But Sir Richard cried in his English pride,
"We have fought such a fight for a day and a
    night
As may never be fought again!
We have won great glory, my men!
And a day less or more
At sea or ashore,
We die—does it matter when?
Sink me the ship, Master Gunner—sink her, split
    her in twain!
Fall into the hands of God, not into the hands of
    Spain!"

And the gunner said, "Ay, ay," but the seamen
    made reply:
"We have children, we have wives,
And the Lord hath spared our lives.
We will make the Spaniard promise, if we yield,
    to let us go;
We shall live to fight again and to strike another
    blow."
And the lion there lay dying, and they yielded to
    the foe.
And the stately Spanish men to their flagship bore
    him then,
Where they laid him by the mast, old Sir Richard
    caught at last,
And they praised him to his face with their
    courtly foreign grace;
But he rose upon their decks, and he cried:
"I have fought for Queen and Faith like a valiant
    man and true;
I have only done my duty as a man is bound to do:
With a joyful spirit I Sir Richard Grenville die!"
And he fell upon their decks, and he died.

And they stared at the dead that had been so
    valiant and true,
And had holden the power and glory of Spain so
    cheap
That he dared her with one little ship and his
    English few;
Was he devil or man? He was devil for aught
    they knew,
But they sank his body with honour down into
    the deep;

o

And they manned the *Revenge* with a swarthier
    alien crew,
And away she sailed with her loss and longed for
    her own;
When a wind from the lands they had ruined
    awoke from sleep,
And the water began to heave and the weather
    to moan,
And or ever that evening ended a great gale blew,
And a wave like the wave that is raised by an
    earthquake grew,
Till it smote on their hulls and their sails and their
    masts and their flags,
And the whole sea plunged and fell on the shot-
    shattered navy of Spain,
And the little *Revenge* herself went down by the
    island crags
To be lost evermore in the main.

                  *Alfred, Lord Tennyson*

### THE ADMIRAL'S GHOST

I TELL you a tale to-night,
    Which a seaman told to me,
With eyes that gleamed in the lanthorn light
    And a voice as low as the sea.

You could almost hear the stars
    Twinkling up in the sky,
And the old wind woke and moaned in the spars,
    And the same old waves went by,

Singing the same old song
　　As ages and ages ago,
While he froze my blood in that deep sea night
　　With the things that he seemed to know.

A bare foot pattered on deck;
　　Ropes creaked; then—all grew still,
And he pointed his finger straight in my face
　　And growled, as a sea-dog will.

"Do 'ee know who Nelson was?
　　That pore little shrivelled form
With the patch on his eye and the pinned-up
　　　　sleeve
　　And a soul like a North Sea storm?

"Ask of the Devonshire men!
　　*They* know and they'll tell you true;
He wasn't the pore little chawed-up chap
　　That Hardy thought he knew.

"He wasn't the man you think!
　　His patch was a dern disguise!
For he knew that they'd find him out, d'you see,
　　If they looked him in both his eyes.

"He was twice as big as he seemed;
　　But his clothes were cunningly made.
He'd both of his hairy arms all right!
　　The sleeve was a trick of the trade.

"You've heard of sperrits, no doubt;
　　Well, there's more in the matter than that!
But he wasn't the patch and he wasn't the sleeve,
　　And he wasn't the laced cocked-hat.

"*Nelson was just—a Ghost!*
    You may laugh!  But the Devonshire men
They knew that he'd come when England called
    And they know that he'll come again.

"I'll tell you the way it was
    (For none of the landsmen know),
And to tell it you right, you must go astarn
    Two hundred years or so.

.            .            .            .            .

"The waves were lapping and slapping
    The same as they are to-day;
And Drake lay dying aboard his ship
    In Nombre Dios Bay.

"The scent of the foreign flowers
    Came floating all around;
'But I'd sell my soul for the smell of the pitch'
    Says he 'in Plymouth Sound.'

" 'What shall I do,' he says,
    'When the guns begin to roar,
An' England wants me, and me not there
    To shatter 'er foes once more?'

("You've heard what he said, maybe,
    But I'll mark you the p'ints again;
For I want you to box your compass right
    And get my story plain.)

" 'You must take my drum,' he says,
    'To the old sea-wall at home;
And if ever you strike that drum,' he says,
    'Why, strike me blind, I'll come!

" 'If England needs me dead
   Or living, I'll rise that day!
I'll rise from the darkness under the sea
   Ten thousand miles away!'

"That's what he said; and he died;
   An' his pirates, listenin' roun'
With their crimson doublets and jewelled swords
   That flashed as the sun went down,

"They sewed him up in his shroud
   With a round-shot top and toe.
They sunk him under the salt sharp sea
   Where all good seamen go.

"They lowered him down in the deep,
   And there in the sunset light
They boomed a broadside over his grave,
   As meanin' to say 'Good-night.'

"They sailed away in the dark
   To the dear little isle they knew;
And they hung his drum by the old sea-wall
   The same as he told them to.

   .     .     .     .     .

"Two hundred years went by,
   And the guns began to roar,
And England was fighting hard for her life,
   As ever she fought of yore.

" 'It's only my dead that count'
   She said, as she says to-day;
'It isn't the ships and it isn't the guns
   'Ull sweep Trafalgar's Bay.'

"D'you guess who Nelson was?
  You may laugh, but it's true as true!
There was more in that pore little chawed-up chap
  Than ever his best friend knew.

"The foe was creepin' close
  In the dark, to our white-cliffed isle;
They were ready to leap at England's throat,
  When—O you may smile, you may smile.

"But ask of the Devonshire men,
  For they heard in the dead of night
The roll of a drum, and they saw *him* pass
  On a ship all shining white.

"He stretched out his dead cold face,
  And he sailed in the grand old way!
The fishes had taken an eye and an arm,
  But he *swept* Trafalgar's Bay.

"Nelson—was Francis Drake!
  O what matters the uniform,
Or the patch on your eye or your pinned-up sleeve,
  If your soul's like a North Sea storm?"

                                        *Alfred Noyes*


### A PRIVATE OF THE BUFFS

*Last night*, among his fellow roughs,
  He jested, quaffed, and swore;
A drunken private of the Buffs,
  Who never looked before.

*To-day*, beneath the foeman's frown,
   He stands in Elgin's place,
Ambassador from Britain's crown,
   And type of all her race.


Poor, reckless, rude, low-born, untaught,
   Bewildered, and alone,
A heart, with English instinct fraught,
   He yet can call his own.
Ay, tear his body limb from limb,
   Bring cord, or axe, or flame,
He only knows that not through him
   Shall England come to shame.


Far Kentish hop-fields round him seemed,
   Like dreams, to come and go;
Bright leagues of cherry-blossom gleamed,
   One sheet of living snow;
The smoke above his father's door
   In grey soft eddyings hung;
Must he then watch it rise no more,
   Doomed by himself, so young?


Yes, honour calls!—with strength like
   steel
   He put the vision by;
Let dusky Indians whine and kneel,
   An English lad must die.
And thus, with eyes that would not shrink,
   With knee to man unbent,
Unfaltering on its dreadful brink,
   To his red grave he went.

Vain, mightiest fleets of iron framed,
  Vain, those all-shattering guns,
Unless proud England keep, untamed,
  The strong heart of her sons.
So let his name through Europe ring—
  A man of mean estate,
Who died, as firm as Sparta's King,
  Because his soul was great.

*Sir Francis Hastings Doyle*

### VITAÏ LAMPADA

THERE's a breathless hush in the Close to-night—
  Ten to make and the match to win—
A bumping pitch and a blinding light,
  An hour to play and the last man in,
And it's not for the sake of a ribboned coat
  Or the selfish hope of a season's fame,
But the Captain's hand on his shoulder smote—
  Play up! play up! and play the game!

The sand of the desert is sodden red—
  Red with the wreck of a square that broke,
The Gatling's jammed and the Colonel dead,
  And the regiment blind with dust and
    smoke
The river of death has brimmed his banks,
  And England's far, and Honour a name,
But the voice of a schoolboy rallies the ranks:
  Play up! play up! and play the game!

This is the word that year by year,
　While in her place the school is set,
Every one of her sons must hear,
　And none that hears it dare forget.
This they all with a joyful mind
　Bear through life, like a torch in flame,
And falling, fling to the host behind—
　Play up! play up! and play the game!

Sir Henry Newbolt

## "FOR ALL WE HAVE AND ARE"

For all we have and are,
For all our children's fate,
Stand up and take the war.
The Hun is at the gate!
Our world has passed away,
In wantonness o'erthrown.
There is nothing left to-day
But steel and fire and stone!
　　Though all we knew depart,
　　The old Commandments stand:—
　　"In courage keep your heart,
　　In strength lift up your hand."

Once more we hear the word
That sickened earth of old:—
"No law except the Sword
Unsheathed and uncontrolled."
Once more it knits mankind,
Once more the nations go

To meet and break and bind
A crazed and driven foe.

Comfort, content, delight,
The ages' slow-bought gain,
They shrivelled in a night:
Only ourselves remain
To face the naked days
In silent fortitude,
Through perils and dismays
Renewed and re-renewed.
    Though all we made depart,
    The old Commandments stand:—
    "In patience keep your heart,
    In strength lift up your hand."

No easy hope or lies
Shall bring us to our goal,
But iron sacrifice
Of body, will, and soul.
There is but one task for all—
One life for each to give.
What stands if Freedom fall?
Who dies if England live?

*Rudyard Kipling*

# IN SERIOUS VEIN

## A MUSICAL INSTRUMENT

WHAT was he doing, the great god Pan,
   Down in the reeds by the river?
Spreading ruin and scattering ban,
Splashing and paddling with hoofs of a goat,
And breaking the golden lilies afloat
   With the dragon-fly on the river.


He tore out a reed, the great god Pan,
   From the deep cool bed of the river;
The limpid water turbidly ran,
And the broken lilies a-dying lay,
And the dragon-fly had fled away,
   Ere he brought it out of the river.


High on the shore sat the great god Pan,
   While turbidly flowed the river;
And hacked and hewed as a great god can
With his hard bleak steel at the patient reed,
Till there was not a sign of the leaf indeed
   To prove it fresh from the river.


He cut it short, did the great god Pan,
   (How tall it stood in the river!),
Then drew the pith, like the heart of a man,
Steadily from the outside ring,
Then notched the poor dry empty thing
   In holes, as he sat by the river.

"This is the way," laughed the great god Pan,
  (Laughed while he sat by the river),
"The only way, since gods began
To make sweet music, they could succeed."
Then, dropping his mouth to a hole in the reed,
  He blew in power by the river.

Sweet, sweet, sweet, O Pan!
  Piercing sweet by the river!
Blinding sweet, O great god Pan!
The sun on the hill forgot to die,
And the lilies revived, and the dragon-fly
  Came back to dream on the river.

Yet half a beast is the great god Pan,
  To laugh as he sits by the river,
Making a poet out of a man:
The true gods sigh for the cost and pain—
For the reed which grows nevermore again
  As a reed with the reeds of the river.

*Elizabeth Barrett Browning*


TUBAL CAIN

Old Tubal Cain was a man of might
  In the days when Earth was young;
By the fierce red light of his furnace bright
  The strokes of his hammer rung;
And he lifted high his brawny hand
  On the iron glowing clear,
Till the sparks rushed out in scarlet showers,
  As he fashioned the sword and spear.

And he sang: "Hurra for my handiwork!
   Hurra for the spear and sword!
Hurra for the hand that shall wield them well,
   For he shall be king and lord!"

To Tubal Cain came many a one,
   As he wrought by his roaring fire,
And each one prayed for a strong steel blade
   As the crown of his desire;
And he made them weapons sharp and strong,
   Till they shouted loud for glee,
And gave him gifts of pearl and gold,
   And spoils of the forest free.
And they sang: "Hurra for Tubal Cain,
   Who has given us strength anew!
Hurra for the smith, hurra for the fire,
   And hurra for the metal true!"

But a sudden change came o'er his heart
   Ere the setting of the sun,
And Tubal Cain was filled with pain
   For the evil he had done;
He saw that men, with rage and hate,
   Made war upon their kind,
That the land was red with the blood they shed,
   In their lust for carnage blind,
And he said: "Alas! that ever I made,
   Or that skill of mine should plan,
The spear and the sword for men whose joy
   Is to slay their fellow-man!"

And for many a day old Tubal Cain
   Sat brooding o'er his woe;

And his hand forbore to smite the ore,
    And his furnace smouldered low.
But he rose at last with a cheerful face,
    And a bright courageous eye,
And bared his strong right arm for work,
    While the quick flames mounted high
And he sang: "Hurra for my handiwork!"
    And the red sparks lit the air;
"Not alone for the blade was the bright steel
        made";
    And he fashioned the first ploughshare.

And men, taught wisdom from the past,
    In friendship joined their hands,
Hung the sword in the hall, the spear on the wall,
    And ploughed the willing lands;
And sang: "Hurra for Tubal Cain!
    Our stanch good friend is he;
And for the ploughshare and the plough
    To him our praise shall be.
But while oppression lifts its head,
    Or a tyrant would be lord,
Though we may thank him for the plough,
    We'll not forget the sword!"

                                    *Charles Mackay*


### THE BALLAD OF FATHER GILLIGAN

THE old priest Peter Gilligan
    Was weary night and day;
For half his flock were in their beds,
    Or under green sods lay.

Once, while he nodded on a chair,
   At the moth-hour of eve,
Another poor man sent for him,
   And he began to grieve.

"I have no rest, nor joy, nor peace,
   For people die and die";
And after cried he, "God forgive!
   My body spake, not I!"

He knelt, and leaning on the chair
   He prayed and fell asleep;
And the moth-hour went from the fields,
   And stars began to peep.

They slowly into millions grew,
   And leaves shook in the wind;
And God covered the world with shade,
   And whispered to mankind.

Upon the time of sparrow chirp
   When the moths came once more,
The old priest Peter Gilligan
   Stood upright on the floor.

"Mavrone, mavrone! the man has died,
   While I slept on the chair";
He roused his horse out of his sleep.
   And rode with little care.

He rode now as he never rode,
   By rocky lane and fen;
The sick man's wife opened the door:
   "Father, you come again!"

"And is the poor man dead?" he cried.
  "He died an hour ago."
The old priest Peter Gilligan
  In grief swayed to and fro.

"When you were gone, he turned and died
  As merry as a bird."
The old priest Peter Gilligan
  He knelt him at the word.

"He who hath made the night of stars
  For souls who tire and bleed,
Sent one of His great angels down
  To help me in my need.

"He who is wrapped in purple robes,
  With planets in His care,
Had pity on the least of things
  Asleep upon a chair."

*W. B. Yeats*